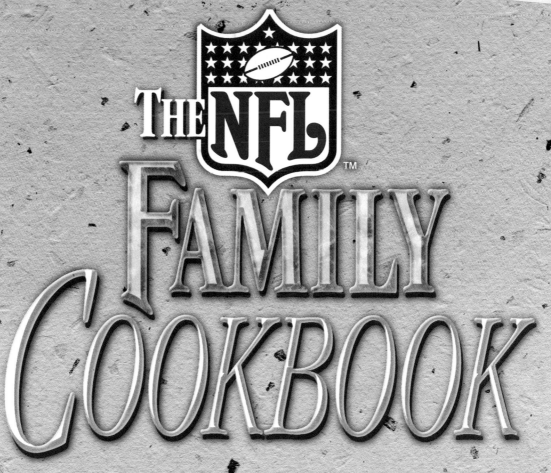

THE NFL FAMILY COOKBOOK

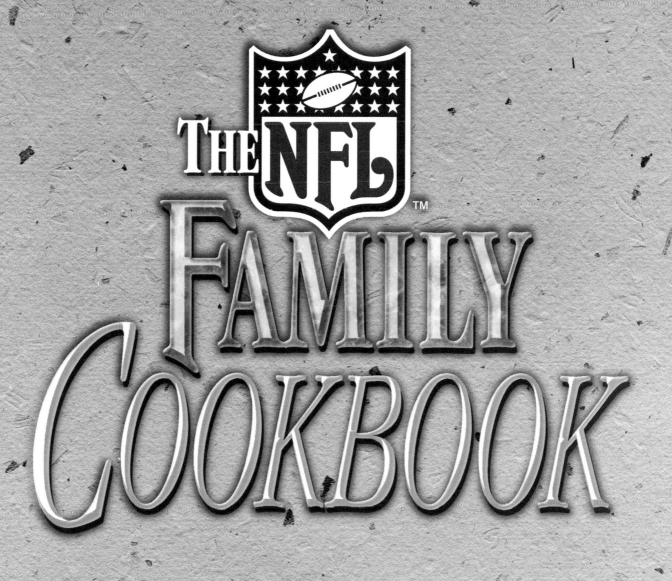

THE NFL FAMILY COOKBOOK

Edited by Jim Natal
Designed by Bill Madrid
NFL Test Kitchen Supervisor Tina Dahl

SMITHMARK

This edition published in 1997 by SMITHMARK Publishers, a division of U.S. Media Holdings,
Inc., 115 W. 18th Street, New York, NY 10011.

SMITHMARK books are available for bulk purchases for sales, promotion, and premium use.
For details, call or write the manager of special sales, SMITHMARK Publishers, 115 W. 18th
Street, New York, NY 10011; (212) 519-1300.

Produced by NFL Properties, Inc., Publishing Group, 6701 Center Drive West, Suite 1111,
Los Angeles, CA 90045.

ISBN 0 7651 9190 3

TABLE OF CONTENTS

PRESEASON

REGULAR SEASON

APPETIZER

*T*here really is an NFL family. It extends from NFL stadiums and playing fields, through club and league offices, and into broadcast booths and studios. The family includes current and former players and coaches, Pro Football Hall of Fame members, club and league executives, broadcasters, print journalists, photographers, and their wives and families—all those who have lived pro football. As Karen Lott, wife of former NFL player Ronnie Lott said, "When you're involved with the NFL, your whole family is involved."

Like any big family (and this is a big family in every sense of the word), this one loves to eat. Food is the essence of family gatherings, and in The NFL Family Cookbook, everyone brings a dish. As you'll see in browsing through the recipe offerings, this is not a gourmet cookbook, but it is not a "down-home" cookbook either. The recipes here range from long-held family secrets to variations on traditional favorites, from restaurant-quality dishes to simple comfort food. Represented here are regional cuisines from places as diverse as the plains of Texas, the bayous of Louisiana, and the beaches of Jamaica and Polynesia. The cooks themselves also are all over the map; some are "scratch cooks," others specialize in just one meal or style of cooking, while still others are schooled chefs with higher culinary aspirations. Then there are the wives and moms who for years have had to get creative at mealtime to satisfy their families.

Have some fun with these recipes. We certainly did that while testing and sampling them. Learning how the NFL eats is just as much an education as learning how it lives. No matter how good a cook you are already, you always can learn a new twist on a familiar dish or ingredient, or pick up a new cooking technique. And, because most cooks rarely make a dish exactly the same way twice, these recipes are as ripe for innovation and experimentation as they are for providing inspiration. Go ahead, try them your way, then add them to your kitchen playbook.

The recipes have been loosely grouped according to the NFL calendar. Offseason, Training Camp, Preseason, Regular Season, and Playoffs correspond to cooking seasonality. For example, you'll find more barbecue fare in the "Preseason" section, tailgating dishes in "Regular Season," hearty soups, stews, and holiday dishes in "Playoffs," and so on. Good cooking knows no special season, but kitchen all-pros know that using seasonal ingredients can improve any recipe. Feel free to substitute fresh herbs for dried and fresh vegetables for canned as the season and availability dictate.

Speaking of substitutions, we recommend using the low-fat, low-sodium versions of products (such as canned soups) whenever possible. And, by all means, cut the sugar and salt in these recipes to taste, or to accommodate any dietary restrictions.

An added bonus of The NFL Family Cookbook is that it provides an opportunity to get to know the members of the extended NFL family in the relaxed settings of their homes and kitchens. These are large people with large appetites and enthusiasms that spill over from the playing field and infuse their lifestyles. They also are nice people—people you'd like to meet. Their food says welcome.

So whether you're a zealous NFL fan, or the only game you watch all season is the Super Bowl, c'mon into the NFL kitchen to see what's cooking.

Jim Natal

OFFSEASON

Earnest Byner
- Grits With Sausage and Eggs

John Elway
- Hamburger Soup

Archie Manning
- Cajun Shrimp Appetizer

Marc Boutte
- Smothered Chicken

Michael Bankston
- Oxtail Stew

Darren Bennett
- Australian Meat Pie

Deacon Jones
- Sweet Potato Pie
- Orange Raisin Glazed Ham
- Cornbread Muffins
- Barbecued Baked Beans
- Deacon's Pork Salad

Howard Mudd
- Spaghetti Casserole

Hardy Nickerson
- Down Home Macaroni and Cheese
- Oatmeal Chocolate Chip Cookies

Dave Szott
- Pasta and Shrimp
- Banana Nut Bread

Australian Meat Pie

Earnest Byner

RUNNING BACK, BALTIMORE RAVENS

Earnest Byner is such a double threat as a runner and receiver that he currently is one of only three players on the NFL's active top 20 lists for rushing yards and receptions. Originally drafted by the Cleveland Browns in 1984, he played in Cleveland for five seasons. Byner then played five seasons with Washington, only to rejoin the Browns in 1994 and make the move to Baltimore in 1996. He ranks sixth on the Browns' career rushing list and third on the Redskins' list.

The Saturday morning breakfast tradition at the Byner household goes something like this: Earnest and his wife Tina get up early and repair to the kitchen to make the family's favorite grits and eggs recipe. "Served with toast and orange juice," Earnest says, "it's quite a filling breakfast." Then Earnest joins his three daughters—Semeria, 13, Adriana Monique, 11, and Brandi, 5—to take in the feast of cartoons that Saturday morning television brings. "I appreciate the time with them," he says.

- 1-2 lbs coarsely ground turkey sausage
- 1 cup grits
- 6-8 eggs, beaten
- 1 cup cheddar cheese, grated

Grits With Sausage and Eggs

1. Prepare the grits according to package directions.
2. Brown the sausage in a large frying pan. Drain any grease from the sausage.
3. Pour the beaten eggs over the sausage. Return the pan to heat and scramble the eggs together with the sausage. Cook until the eggs are done.
4. Spoon the grits into individual serving bowls. Top the grits first with the egg-sausage mixture, then a sprinkling of cheedar cheese. Serve hot.

John Elway

QUARTERBACK, DENVER BRONCOS

No lead is safe when Elway is playing. In 1996, Elway engineered the forty-first comeback drive of his remarkable career with Denver. Elway also joined Dan Marino and Fran Tarkenton as the only quarterbacks in NFL history to surpass 45,000 career passing yards. In his 14 seasons with the Broncos, Elway has led them to three Super Bowls. He was named the NFL's most valuable player by *Associated Press* in 1987.

"This is a quick and easy soup that's a real favorite in our family," Elway says. "We enjoy it often at home. It makes a great meal served with warm bread."

- 2-3 lbs lean hamburger
- 1-2 medium onions, chopped
- 1 clove garlic, minced
- 2 Tbs butter
- 3 cans (10¾ oz each) beef broth
- 2 cans (10 oz each) diced tomatoes with green chiles
- 1 medium can (15 oz) tomato sauce
- 1 cup potatoes, diced (with skin)
- 1 cup carrots, diced
- 1 cup celery, diced
- 1 can (14½ oz) french-style green beans
- 1 cup dry red wine
- 1 Tbs parsley, minced
- ½ tsp basil
- salt and pepper, to taste

Hamburger Soup

1. In a large frying pan, brown the hamburger and crumble into small pieces. Drain the grease and set aside.

2. In a large soup pot, sauté the onions and garlic in the butter until the onions begin to color.

3. Add the hamburger meat to the pot, then add all the other ingredients. Stir well. Bring the pot to a boil, then reduce heat. Simmer the soup until the vegetables are tender, about 30-40 minutes.

Archie Manning

QUARTERBACK, NEW ORLEANS SAINTS (1971-75, 1977-1982), HOUSTON OILERS (1982-83), MINNESOTA VIKINGS (1983-84)
Archie Manning is a bayou legend despite playing on underachieving teams. He had his best statistical season in 1980, passing for 3,716 yards and 23 touchdowns. He still holds the Saints' career records for passing yardage (21,734) and touchdowns (115). The Saints made Manning the second overall pick in the 1971 NFL draft, following his standout career at the University of Mississippi.

Archie Manning and his wife Olivia both are Mississippi natives, but have lived in southern Louisiana most of the 26 years they have been married. "The food down here is hard to beat," says Archie. "It'll spoil you." This Cajun Shrimp Appetizer recipe is one of their favorites for tailgating. "This is a very popular dish when Olivia makes it," he says. "But she keeps a low profile about her cooking skill. I think she's afraid of what would happen if she got the reputation of being a good cook."

- 6 lbs raw shrimp in the shell
- 2 bay leaves
- 1 Tbs celery seed
- ¾ cup salt
- 1 tsp cayenne pepper
- 2 cups vegetable oil
- ½ cup ketchup
- 3 Tbs lemon juice
- ¼ cup apple-cider vinegar
- 1 Tbs Worcestershire sauce
- 1 jar (5 oz) horseradish
- 1 jar (5 oz) hot creole mustard
- 1 cup yellow onion, thinly sliced
- salt and pepper, to taste

Cajun Shrimp Appetizer

1. Put the shrimp in a large pot and cover with water. Add bay leaves, celery seed, salt, and cayenne. Bring to a boil and cook five minutes, until shrimp are pink. Drain and peel.
2. Combine remaining ingredients. Add cooked shrimp and toss to coat. Cover and refrigerate.

 EXTRA POINT: This recipe should be prepared one day ahead for best flavor. Serve in a lettuce-lined bowl with party toothpicks or crackers.

Marc Boutte

DEFENSIVE TACKLE, WASHINGTON REDSKINS

Marc Boutte has gained his own cheering section at Redskins' games since he came to Washington in 1994. A third-round draft choice by the Los Angeles Rams in 1992, he played two seasons for the Rams before signing with the Redskins. In 1995, Boutte's 70 tackles led all Washington linemen, and he made his first career pass interception in 1996.

"I guess you can call this a family recipe," Boutte says. "I've been watching my mother make it since I was a youngster." Boutte has plans to open a restaurant in the next year or two in the Lake Charles area in southern Louisiana, where he grew up and where he lives during the offseason. He says his favorite pastime these days is watching cooking shows on television to learn new cooking styles and techniques. Boutte's wife, Tananjalyn, a world-class competitor in the hurdles, is from northern Louisiana. "It's a whole different world up there," Marc says. "They cook southern-style and soul food. It's good, but I like cooking Cajun."

Smothered Chicken

1. Rub the chicken with prepared Cajun seasoning mix (available in the spice sections of most large supermarkets). Heat the oil in a large, heavy pot or frying pan. Brown the chicken on all sides, and remove from the pot.
2. Pour off all but about 1-2 tsp of the oil, leaving brown bits from the chicken in the bottom of the pot. Saute vegetables in the remaining oil until tender.
3. Return the chicken to the pot on top of the vegetables. Mix the flour and water well, then pour into the pot. Cover and cook 1 hour, stirring occasionally. Correct the seasoning and serve.

- Cajun seasoning mix
- 1 chicken, cut up
- ½ cup vegetable oil
- 1 onion, chopped
- 1 green bell pepper, chopped
- 1 green onion, chopped
- 1 jalapeño pepper, minced
- 1 tsp flour
- 1 cup water

Michael Bankston

DEFENSIVE END, ARIZONA CARDINALS

Michael Bankston, who can play both defensive tackle and defensive end, has added a powerful dimension to the Arizona defense. In 1996, he started all 16 games at left end, the third consecutive season he started every game. Bankston led all Arizona defensive linemen in tackles each season from 1993-95. After a standout college career at Sam Houston State, Bankston was selected by the Cardinals in the fourth round of the 1992 NFL draft.

Bankston loves this oxtail stew. "My wife, Kimberly, got the recipe from her mother down in southeastern Texas," he says. "I like to eat it the southern way, with cornbread crumbled on top." In the Bankston home, Kimberly does the "special" cooking; Michael is in charge of barbecuing and frying catfish. "When we have the oxtail stew," he says, "I eat it out of a large bowl that Kimberly always kids me about. She calls it my 'Herman Munster' bowl."

- 3-4 lbs beef oxtail
- salt and pepper to taste
- 3 large potatoes
- 1 package (2 lbs.) frozen mixed vegetables
- 1 can (14½ oz.) beef broth
- 3-5 bay leaves

Oxtail Stew

1. Season the oxtail sections with salt and pepper. Boil in water until tender, 1½-2 hours (or longer, if necessary), skimming fat from surface occasionally.

2. When oxtails are tender, peel the potatoes and cut into wedges. Add to the pot with the oxtails. Add the vegetables and beef broth and cook another hour.

3. When the potatoes are done, add the bay leaves. Simmer another 20-30 minutes and serve.

Kimberly amd Michael Bankston

Darren Bennett

PUNTER, SAN DIEGO CHARGERS

Darren Bennett, originally an Australian Rules Football player with the Perth West Coast Eagles and the Melbourne Demons, signed with San Diego in 1994. He spent one season on the Chargers' practice squad and one season in the World League with the Amsterdam Admirals before earning a spot on San Diego's roster. In 1995, he was voted to the Pro Bowl, becoming the first player ever named to both the Pro Bowl and the all-World League first team.

Darren and Rosemary Bennett like to cook Australian when they entertain. "We like to make dishes our American friends don't usually see," Darren says. "But one thing we don't do for them is 'throw a shrimp on the barbie.' It just screws up the grill." The roots of the Australian meat pie they share here developed from a "winter farmer's meal," says Darren. "But in a smaller form, kind of like an American pot pie, it is a snack. Meat pies are our traditional food at sporting events, the way people here eat hot dogs."

Australian Meat Pie

- 2 lbs round steak
- ¼ cup flour
- salt and pepper
- 2 Tbs vegetable oil
- 1 medium onion, chopped
- 1 cup beef stock
- 2 Tbs tomato paste
- 1 Tbs Worcestershire sauce
- 12-oz frozen puff pastry, thawed
- 1 egg, lightly beaten for glazing

1. Trim any excess fat from the steak, then cut steak into one-inch cubes. Add salt and pepper to the flour and place in a plastic bag; shake well to mix. Add the cubed meat to the bag and toss gently until the meat is well coated with flour. Remove the meat, shaking off any excess flour.

2. Heat the oil in a heavy skillet and add the meat in batches, cooking the meat quickly until browned. Drain the meat on paper towels. Add the onion to the pan and cook for five minutes, or until soft.

3. Return the meat to the pan. Then add the stock, tomato paste, and Worcestershire sauce and bring to boil. Reduce the heat and simmer, covered, for 90 minutes, stirring occasionally. Remove the pan from the heat. Cool completely.

4. Preheat oven to 400 degrees. Transfer the meat mixture to a four-cup capacity pie dish.

5. Roll out the pastry until it is one-eighth-inch thick. Place the pastry over the pie and trim, allowing enough excess dough to completely overlap the edges of the dish. Press the pastry around the edges of dish to seal the edges tightly. Use leftover pastry to decorate the top of the pie.

6. Brush the top of the pie with the beaten egg and bake for 30 minutes, or until golden brown.

Darren and Rosemary Bennett in the kitchen with William Cole

Deacon Jones

DEFENSIVE END, LOS ANGELES RAMS (1961-1971), SAN DIEGO CHARGERS (1972-73), WASHINGTON REDSKINS (1974)

David (Deacon) Jones was a member of the Rams' legendary "Fearsome Foursome" defensive line, using his trademark "head slap" to intimidate offensive linemen. Jones, credited as the originator of the term "sack," was inducted into the Pro Football Hall of Fame in 1980. He was voted to nine Pro Bowls, and was selected to the NFL's 75th Anniversary team at defensive end in 1994.

Deacon is a cook on a mission and many of his recipes are top secret. "This is the first time Deacon's ever given out his recipe for the barbecued baked beans," Elizabeth Jones says. "It was such a secret that, for a while, he wouldn't even let me go to the store to buy the ingredients. He really is an excellent cook. He used to do all the cooking when we first got married—until he taught me how he liked things cooked. It was great. I had my own business then, and I'd come home to a wonderful meal. I figured out why men like having good wives."

Sweet Potato Pie

1. Preheat oven to 375 degrees. In a large mixing bowl, combine the sweet potatoes, brown sugar, milk, and whipping cream. Beat until smooth.

2. Add the eggs one at a time, beating well after each is added.

3. Add the bourbon, butter, spices, and salt. Beat until well blended.

4. Pour the sweet potato mixture into the pastry shell. Bake the pie for 50-55 minutes, or until set. Cool and garnish with whipped cream.

- 1 can (17-oz) sweet potatoes, drained and mashed
- 1 cup brown sugar, firmly packed
- ⅔ cup milk
- ⅔ cup whipping cream
- 3 eggs
- 3 Tbs bourbon
- 1 Tbs butter, melted
- 1 tsp ground cinnamon
- ½ tsp ground nutmeg
- ½ tsp ground ginger
- ¼ tsp salt
- 1 9-inch pastry shell (deep dish)
- whipped cream for garnish

Orange Raisin Glazed Ham

1. Preheat oven to 325 degrees. Place the ham in a roasting pan and bake for 30 minutes per pound.

2. While the ham is baking, prepare the glaze. In a small saucepan, mix the water, orange juice, cornstarch, allspice, cinnamon, and salt, stirring until smooth. Heat, stirring constantly, until the mixture thickens and boils. Add the orange marmalade and raisins. Continue stirring until the marmalade melts and the raisins become soft.

3. Baste the ham thoroughly with the orange raisin glaze several times during the last 1-1½ hours of cooking. The glaze should be thick and caramelized when the ham is done.

- 1 7-8 lb bone-in ham, fresh or smoked
- 1 cup water
- ⅔ cup orange juice
- 2 Tbs cornstarch
- ⅛ tsp allspice
- ⅛ tsp cinnamon
- ⅛ tsp salt
- ½ cup orange marmalade
- ¼ cup white raisins
- ¼ cup black raisins

- 2 cups yellow corn meal
- 1 ½ cups all-purpose flour
- 2-4 Tbs sugar (to taste)
- 2 Tbs baking powder
- 1 tsp salt
- 4 eggs, slightly beaten
- 1 ½ cups milk
- ⅔ cup vegetable oil

Cornbread Muffins

1. Preheat oven to 375 degrees. Grease 2 muffin tins (8 muffins each). Set aside.

2. In a large mixing bowl, stir together the dry ingredients. Add the eggs, milk, and oil and mix well.

3. Pour the cornmeal batter into greased muffin tins, filling each section about half full. Bake for 25-30 minutes, or until golden brown. Serve hot with butter and honey.

Orange Raisin Glazed Ham

Barbecued Baked Beans

- 1 large (or 4 small) smoked link sausage
- 2 cans (28 oz each) baked beans
- 1 large onion, diced
- 1-2 cups brown sugar (to taste)
- ½ cup water
- ¼ cup cinnamon
- ½ tsp coarse red pepper flakes

1. Cook the sausage thoroughly. Chop coarsely.

2. Prepare the barbecue coals. Combine the sausage with all other ingredients in a large cast iron Dutch oven or other pot that can be placed directly on the barbecue.

3. Place the pot, uncovered, on the barbecue grate. Close the barbecue lid and allow the beans to smoke 20 minutes or more before serving.

Deacon's Pork Salad

1. Boil the ham hocks in adequate water until tender.

2. Meanwhile, soak the collard greens in water and wash several times until clean. Remove the stems and the center veins from the leaves, then cut the leaves into small pieces.

2. Place the greens in a large pot with the cooked ham hocks. Add the onion, peppers, bacon, one cup water, and salt. Bring pot to a boil, then cover and reduce heat to low. Cook for 1-1½ hours, or until the greens are tender.

- 3 small lean ham hocks, smoked or fresh
- 6 bunches collard greens
- 1 Tbs lard, bacon fat, or vegetable oil
- 1 onion, finely chopped
- 2 jalapeño peppers, diced
- 4 slices lean, thick-cut, smoked bacon
- 1 cup water
- 1 tsp salt

EXTRA POINT: According to Elizabeth Jones, these recipes "make dinner for eight football players or 16 normal people. Except for the pie—and you'd better make two of them."

Howard Mudd

OFFENSIVE LINE COACH, SEATTLE SEAHAWKS

Howard Mudd played seven years in the NFL as a guard for the San Francisco 49ers (1964-1969) and the Chicago Bears (1969-1970). After retiring as a player, he became an assistant coach, joining the Seahawks' coaching staff in 1978 after stints in San Diego and San Francisco. Mudd went on to coach the offensive lines of the Cleveland Browns and Kansas City Chiefs before returning to Seattle in 1993.

Mudd says his Spaghetti Casserole was a happy accident. "I was playing around with the idea of layering spaghetti to give it a lasagna kind of treatment. Now it's a real favorite around my house, and we make it on a regular basis." Mudd invested considerable time and effort perfecting his original recipes. "I remember back in my playing days calling my mother long distance," he says, "and having her talk me through making a crust for an apple pie." Mudd recently completed a gourmet cooking course. "It was a serious course," he says. "For example, we spent one entire session just on the properties of oils and vinegars. Now I make all my own salad dressings from scratch."

Spaghetti Casserole

1. Remove the sausage meat from the casings. Fry the sausage meat and the onion in olive oil until the sausage crumbles and the onion is soft. Add just enough marinara sauce to the sausage and onion to make a thick mixture.

2. Cook and drain the pasta following package directions.

3. Preheat oven to 375 degrees. Cover the bottom of a deep baking dish with a layer of cooked pasta. Cover the pasta with a thin layer of the sauce and sausage mixture. Add a thin layer of cottage cheese next. Sprinkle bread crumbs over the cottage cheese. Cover the bread crumbs with a layer of mozzarella. Then repeat the layers, making sure that mozzarella is the layer at the top.

4. Bake covered for 45 minutes. Remove the cover and bake for another 15 minutes to give the casserole a nice crust.

- **1 lb Italian sausage (spicy or mild, to taste)**
- **1 large onion, coarsely chopped**
- **1 Tbs olive oil**
- **1-2 cups marinara sauce, homemade or prepared**
- **1 lb angel hair pasta**
- **1 pint small curd cottage cheese**
- **Italian bread crumbs**
- **1 lb mozzarella cheese, grated**

EXTRA POINT: To make a vegetarian version of this recipe, substitute green peppers and mushrooms for the sausage. Use hot red-pepper flakes to add spiciness, if desired.

Hardy Nickerson

LINEBACKER, TAMPA BAY BUCCANEERS

Nickerson is the cornerstone of a resurgent Tampa Bay defense. Nickerson joined the Buccaneers in 1993 and led the team in tackles for the next three seasons. He was named to his second Pro Bowl following the 1996 season. Nickerson was drafted by the Pittsburgh Steelers in the fifth round in 1987.

Hardy's wife Amy says her Oatmeal Chocolate Chip Cookies don't last long once Hardy and their three children smell them in the oven.

- 2 sticks butter or margarine
- 1 cup granulated sugar
- 1 cup brown sugar
- 2 eggs
- 1 tsp vanilla
- 1 tsp baking soda
- ½ tsp salt
- 2 cups quick oats (not instant)
- 2¾ cups flour
- 1 cup chocolate chips
- ½ cup pecans, chopped (optional)

Oatmeal Chocolate Chip Cookies

1. Preheat oven to 325 degrees.
2. In a large bowl, blend the butter, sugar, and eggs. Add the vanilla, baking soda, and salt and mix well.
3. Slowly add the oats, flour, chocolate chips, and nuts until mixed well.
4. Drop the dough by rounded spoonfuls onto ungreased cookie sheets (about two inches apart). Bake for 11-13 minutes, or until golden brown. Remove cookies with a spatula and cool on plates or a wire rack.

*Nickerson shows off
the new Buccaneers uniform.*

Down-Home
Macaroni and Cheese

1. Preheat oven to 350 degrees.

2. In a large pot, cook the macaroni according to package instructions. Drain and
   return to the pot. Quickly stir in the butter and salt.

3. In a separate bowl, combine the beaten eggs and evaporated milk.

4. Grease a casserole dish with butter. Layer the macaroni and the cheese in the
   dish in alternating layers, ending with cheese. Pour the egg mixture over the
   entire dish.

5. Bake uncovered for 45 minutes.

- 4 cups uncooked
  macaroni
- ¼ cup butter, softened
- 2 Tbs salt
- 3 large eggs, beaten
- 2 cups evaporated milk
- 1-1 ½ lbs sharp cheddar
  cheese, grated

Dave Szott

GUARD, KANSAS CITY CHIEFS

Dave Szott was a seventh-round draft choice by Kansas City in 1990 who has developed into one of the best guards in the NFL. In 1996, he started all 16 games for the Chiefs at left guard for the fifth time in six years. Szott's dependable play has helped anchor the Kansas City offense, which led the NFL with 2,222 rushing yards in 1995 and ranked fourth in 1996.

- ½ cup Italian salad dressing
- ½ lb medium shrimp, peeled and deveined
- 1 medium yellow squash, cut into julienne strips
- 1 medium zucchini, cut into julienne strips
- 1 carrot, cut into julienne strips
- 3 green onions, cut into thin strips
- 2 tsp grated lemon peel
- 1 clove garlic, minced (or more to taste)
- 1 tsp salt (or to taste)
- dash of cayenne pepper (optional)
- ½ lb pasta (angel hair or linguine suggested)
- ¼ cup parsley, finely chopped
- Parmesan cheese, grated
- freshly ground black pepper (optional)

Pasta and Shrimp

1. In a medium skillet, heat the Italian dressing over medium heat. Add the shrimp, vegetables, lemon peel, garlic, salt, and optional cayenne. Cook, stirring, 8-10 minutes.

2. Cook the pasta according to package directions. Drain and place in a large serving bowl.

3. Pour the shrimp-vegetable mixture over the pasta and gently toss.

4. Sprinkle with the parsley, grated Parmesan, and the optional pepper. Serve hot.

Banana Nut Bread

1. Preheat oven to 350 degrees.

2. In a large mixing bowl, cream together the butter and sugar.

3. Add the eggs and mix well. Blend in the bananas, then gradually add the flour and the baking soda. Stir in the nuts.

4. Bake in a greased loaf pan for one hour. Cool and slice.

- ½ cup butter or margarine
- 1 cup sugar
- 2 eggs
- 3 medium bananas, mashed
- 2 cups flour, sifted
- 1 tsp baking soda
- ¼ cup walnut pieces (or other nuts)

 EXTRA POINT: This tasty banana-nut loaf from Dave Szott's wife Andrea is easy to make and is a good way to use overripe bananas.

Pro Football Hall of Fame

Herb Adderley, defensive back

Lance Alworth, wide receiver

Doug Atkins, defensive end

Morris (Red) Badgro, end

Lem Barney, cornerback

Cliff Battles, halfback

Sammy Baugh, quarterback

Chuck Bednarik, center, linebacker

Bert Bell, team owner, Commissioner

Bobby Bell, linebacker

Raymond Berry, end

Charles W. Bidwill, Sr., team owner

Fred Biletnikoff, wide receiver

George Blanda, quarterback, kicker

Mel Blount, cornerback

Terry Bradshaw, quarterback

Jim Brown, fullback

Paul Brown, coach

Roosevelt Brown, tackle

Willie Brown, cornerback

Buck Buchanan, defensive tackle

Dick Butkus, linebacker

Earl Campbell, running back

Tony Canadeo, halfback

Joe Carr, NFL president

Guy Chamberlin, end, coach

Jack Christiansen, safety

Earl (Dutch) Clark, quarterback

George Connor, tackle, linebacker

Jimmy Conzelman, quarterback, coach

Lou Creekmur, tackle, guard

Larry Csonka, running back

Al Davis, coach, team and league administrator

Willie Davis, defensive end

Len Dawson, quarterback

Dan Dierdorf, tackle

Mike Ditka, tight end

Art Donovan, defensive tackle

Tony Dorsett, running back

John (Paddy) Driscoll, quarterback

Bill Dudley, halfback

Albert Glen (Turk) Edwards, tackle

Weeb Ewbank, coach

Tom Fears, end

Jim Finks, administrator

Ray Flaherty, coach

Len Ford, defensive end

Dan Fortmann, guard

Dan Fouts, quarterback

Frank Gatski, center

Bill George, linebacker

Joe Gibbs, coach

Frank Gifford, halfback

Sid Gillman, coach

Otto Graham, quarterback

Harold (Red) Grange, halfback

Bud Grant, coach

Joe Greene, defensive tackle

Forrest Gregg, tackle

Bob Griese, quarterback

Lou Groza, tackle, kicker

Joe Guyon, halfback

George Halas, end, coach, team owner

Jack Ham, linebacker

John Hannah, guard

Franco Harris, running back

Mike Haynes, cornerback

Ed Healey, tackle

Mel Hein, center

Ted Hendricks, linebacker

Wilbur (Pete) Henry, tackle

Arnie Herber, quarterback

Bill Hewitt, end

Clarke Hinkle, fullback

Elroy (Crazylegs) Hirsch, halfback, end

Paul Hornung, halfback

Ken Houston, safety

Cal Hubbard, tackle

Sam Huff, linebacker

Lamar Hunt, team owner

Don Hutson, end

Jimmy Johnson, cornerback

John Henry Johnson, fullback

Charlie Joiner, wide receiver
David (Deacon) Jones, defensive end
Stan Jones, guard,
defensive tackle
Henry Jordan, defensive tackle
Sonny Jurgensen, quarterback
Leroy Kelly, running back
Walt Kiesling, guard, coach
Frank (Bruiser) Kinard, tackle
Earl (Curly) Lambeau, coach
Jack Lambert, linebacker
Tom Landry, coach
Dick (Night Train) Lane, cornerback
Jim Langer, center
Willie Lanier, linebacker
Steve Largent, wide receiver
Yale Lary, defensive back, punter
Dante Lavelli, end
Bobby Layne, quarterback
Alphonse (Tuffy) Leemans, fullback
Bob Lilly, defensive tackle
Larry Little, guard
Vince Lombardi, coach
Sid Luckman, quarterback
William Roy (Link) Lyman, tackle
John Mackey, tight end
Tim Mara, team owner
Wellington Mara, team owner
Gino Marchetti, defensive end
George Preston Marshall,
team owner
Ollie Matson, halfback
Don Maynard, wide receiver
George McAfee, halfback
Mike McCormack, tackle
Hugh McElhenny, halfback
Johnny (Blood) McNally, halfback
Mike Michalske, guard

Wayne Millner, end
Bobby Mitchell, running back,
wide receiver
Ron Mix, tackle
Lenny Moore, flanker, running back
Marion Motley, fullback
George Musso, guard, tackle
Bronko Nagurski, fullback
Joe Namath, quarterback
Earle (Greasy) Neale, coach
Ernie Nevers, fullback
Ray Nitschke, linebacker
Chuck Noll, coach
Leo Nomellini, defensive tackle
Merlin Olsen, defensive tackle
Jim Otto, center
Steve Owen, tackle, coach
Alan Page, defensive tackle
Clarence (Ace) Parker, quarterback
Jim Parker, guard, tackle
Walter Payton, running back
Joe Perry, fullback
Pete Pihos, end
Hugh (Shorty) Ray, supervisor
of officials
Dan Reeves, team owner
Mel Renfro, cornerback, safety
John Riggins, running back
Jim Ringo, center
Andy Robustelli, defensive end
Art Rooney, team owner
Pete Rozelle, Commissioner
Bob St. Clair, tackle
Gale Sayers, running back
Joe Schmidt, linebacker
Tex Schramm, team president,
general manager
Lee Roy Selmon, defensive end

Art Shell, tackle
Don Shula, coach
O.J. Simpson, running back
Jackie Smith, tight end
Bart Starr, quarterback
Roger Staubach, quarterback
Ernie Stautner, defensive tackle
Jan Stenerud, kicker
Ken Strong, halfback
Joe Stydahar, tackle
Fran Tarkenton, quarterback
Charley Taylor, running back,
wide receiver
Jim Taylor, fullback
Jim Thorpe, halfback
Y.A. Tittle, quarterback
George Trafton, center
Charley Trippi, halfback
Emlen Tunnell, safety
Clyde (Bulldog) Turner, center
Johnny Unitas, quarterback
Gene Upshaw, guard
Norm Van Brocklin, quarterback
Steve Van Buren, halfback
Doak Walker, halfback
Bill Walsh, coach
Paul Warfield, wide receiver
Bob Waterfield, quarterback
Mike Webster, center
Arnie Weinmeister,
defensive tackle
Randy White, defensive tackle
Bill Willis, guard
Larry Wilson, safety
Kellen Winslow, tight end
Alex Wojciechowicz, center
Willie Wood, safety

TRAINING CAMP

Bobby Beathard
- Good and Hearty Bran Muffins

Tom Coughlin
- Fried Cakes
- Vegetable Pizza
- Beef Pot Roast
- Apple Bundt Cake

Tommy Brasher
- Low-Fat Eggplant Parmesan

Rodney Hampton
- Baked Chicken

Dave Wannstedt
- Beef Flautas

Jeff Fisher
- Barbecued Pork Tenderloin
- Party Lobsters

Dermontti Dawson
- Chicken Parmesan

Manu Tuiasosopo
- Kalua Pig Roast

Gale Sayers
- Texas Caviar
- Yeast Rolls

Steve Young
- Sherry's Chocolate Chip Cookies

Lamar Hunt
- Jonesey's Strawberry Cake

Lindy Infante
- Crunchy Coffee Frozen Torte

Vegetable Pizza

Bobby Beathard

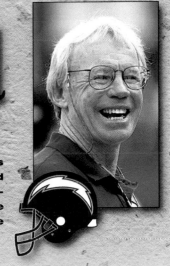

GENERAL MANAGER, SAN DIEGO CHARGERS

Bobby Beathard, one of the NFL's savviest executives, began his career as a scout for the Kansas City Chiefs and Atlanta Falcons before he was named director of player personnel for the Miami Dolphins in 1972. Beathard became general manager of the Washington Redskins in 1978. He joined the San Diego Chargers in 1990. He has had a hand in six teams that have reached the Super Bowl, three at Washington.

From their active southern California lifestyle, you never would guess Bobby and Christine Beathard have four grown children and eight grandchildren. Bobby and Christine both are runners, and Bobby also is an avid cyclist and surfer. "The last time I touched a surfboard," Christine says with a laugh, "I was fifteen years old." The Beathards' diet reflects their lifestyle. "We don't eat health food exclusively," Christine says, "we just eat healthy food. Bobby doesn't eat red meat, but he enjoys fish and chicken once in a while. We make dishes with rice, beans, and whole grains, and eat a lot of soups and vegetables. There are so many good vegetarian cookbooks out now, it makes healthy cooking creative and fun. I love it."

Good and Hearty Bran Muffins

1. In a large bowl, stir the boiling water into the bran cereal. Let cool.

2. In a separate bowl, beat the eggs. Add oil, brown sugar, and buttermilk.

3. Combine the egg-oil mixture with the cereal and mix well.

4. In another large mixing bowl, combine the flour, spices, baking soda, baking powder, salt, raisins, and granola. Mix well.

5. Mix together the contents of the two bowls, stirring until the dry ingredients are well moistened. Cover and refrigerate overnight.

6. Preheat oven to 375 degrees. Spoon the batter into greased muffin tins. Fill each cup half to two-thirds full. Bake for 18-22 minutes, or until a toothpick inserted into the center of a muffin comes out clean.

- 1 ¼ cups all-bran cereal
- 1 cup boiling water
- ½ cup vegetable oil
- ¾ cup brown sugar, firmly packed
- 2 eggs
- 2 cups buttermilk
- 2 cups whole wheat flour
- ½ tsp nutmeg
- 1 tsp cinnamon
- 2 tsp baking soda
- ½ tsp baking powder
- ½ tsp salt
- 1 cup raisins
- 2 cups granola (plain, or with fruit and nuts), OR 1 cup oatmeal and 1 cup *unprocessed* bran

 EXTRA POINT: This recipe makes about 22 muffins. Bake only as many as you need for a day or two; extra batter may be refrigerated and used within two weeks.

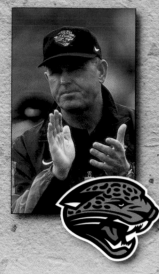

Tom Coughlin

HEAD COACH, JACKSONVILLE JAGUARS

Coughlin built the Jaguars from scratch and then coached them to within one game of Super Bowl XXXI in the team's second season. Before taking on the challenge of shaping the expansion Jaguars, Coughlin was the head coach at Boston College (1991-93) and, before that, was an NFL assistant with Philadelphia, Green Bay, and the New York Giants. Coughlin, a former halfback at Syracuse (1965-67), played in the same backfield as future NFL greats Larry Csonka and Floyd Little.

"With a family of four kids and Tom's hectic schedule, if a dish takes more than an hour to prepare it doesn't stay in my recipe box long." So says Judy Coughlin, wife of the Jacksonville Jaguars' busy coach. "Two of the recipes here are mine—the Apple Bundt Cake, which is Tom's favorite, and the easy-to-make Vegetable Pizza. The cake recipe actually is from a neighbor who lived next door to our first house in Victor, New York. She used to pick the apples for the cake off her backyard tree. The Beef Pot Roast recipe comes from Tom's mother, Betty, who is a great cook and my kitchen inspiration." The Fried Cakes recipe is handed down from Tom's grandmother. "We've all made them," Judy says, "but nobody makes them like she did."

- 3 eggs
- 3 cups granulated sugar
- 2 cups warm mashed potatoes
- 3 Tbs butter, melted
- ½ tsp baking soda
- 1 cup sour milk (or buttermilk)
- 1 tsp salt
- 4 tsp baking powder
- 1 tsp nutmeg
- ½ tsp cinnamon
- 5-6 cups unbleached flour
- vegetable oil for frying

Fried Cakes

1. Beat the eggs. Beat in the sugar, then the mashed potatoes. Add the butter.

2. Stir the baking soda into the milk. Add the salt, baking powder, nutmeg, and cinnamon and mix well. Blend into the potato mixture.

3. Work the flour into the potato mixture. Roll out the dough in sections, one-half-inch thick. Form the dough into doughnut shapes.

4. Pour oil about 1-inch deep in a heavy medium-sized frying pan and heat to 370 degrees. Test the temperature with a doughnut-hole sized dough ball—it should rise to the surface of the oil and come out clean. Brown the cakes in the oil. Drain and serve.

Tom and Judy Coughlin juggle busy schedules to prepare Apple Bundt Cake.

Vegetable Pizza

1. Preheat oven to 375 degrees. Spread the crescent rolls out on large flat baking pan or cookie sheet. Bake for 5 to 7 minutes until golden brown. Let the crust cool completely.

2. Combine the cream cheese, mayonnaise, and dressing and mix well. Spread the mixture over the crust.

3. Refrigerate. Top the crust with the vegetables just before serving.

- 1 package refrigerated crescent rolls
- 1 8-oz package cream cheese
- ½ cup mayonnaise
- ½-¾ envelope ranch dressing
- your choice of chopped vegetables (for example: thinly sliced sweet red peppers, sliced sugar snap peas, and chopped chives)

Beef Pot Roast

- 4-5 lbs beef chuck, round, or rump
- ¼ cup flour
- 3 Tbs vegetable oil
- salt and pepper, to taste
- 1 ½ cups water
- 1 lb small white or red potatoes, peeled and quartered
- 3-4 carrots, peeled and sliced into 1-inch sections
- 2 medium onions, quartered
- ¼ cup prepared white horseradish

1. Dust the meat with flour to coat. In a large, heavy pot, brown the meat on all sides in the oil.

2. Season the meat with salt and pepper. Add the water. Cover and cook slowly for 3 to 4 hours. As liquid cooks away, add more as necessary.

3. Add the uncooked vegetables to the pot approximately 1 hour before the meat is done. Cover and finish cooking over medium heat. When the vegetables are tender, add the horseradish and stir.

Apple Bundt Cake

- 6 apples, pared, cored, and sliced
- ⅓ cup + 2 cups sugar
- 1 ½ tsp cinnamon
- ¾ tsp nutmeg
- 3 cups flour
- 3 tsp baking powder
- 1 tsp salt
- 1 cup vegetable oil
- 4 eggs
- ¼ cup orange juice
- 1 Tbs vanilla

1. Preheat oven to 325 degrees. In a large bowl, mix together 6 cups of apples, one-third cup of the sugar, cinnamon, and nutmeg. Set aside.

2. In another bowl, mix together the flour, the remaining 2 cups of sugar, the baking powder and the salt. Make a well in the center of the mixture and add oil, eggs, orange juice, and vanilla. Beat with a mixing spoon until the batter is thick and blended well.

3. Spoon the batter into a well-greased bundt pan, alternately layering the batter with the apples, ending with batter on top.

4. Bake for 1 hour, 15 minutes. Cool and glaze, if desired.

 EXTRA POINT: This recipe also works well with fruits other than apples, such as peaches or plums.

Tommy Brasher

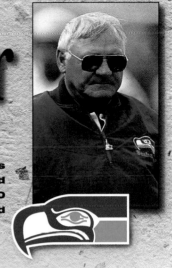

DEFENSIVE LINE COACH, SEATTLE SEAHAWKS

Tommy Brasher was a linebacker for Arkansas in 1962 and 1963 and was a teammate of Dallas Cowboys owner Jerry Jones and Miami Dolphins head coach Jimmy Johnson. He began his coaching career at Arkansas in 1970 before landing his first NFL job as defensive line coach of the New England Patriots in 1982. He joined the Seahawks in 1992.

Tommy Brasher is no stranger to old-fashioned high-fat cooking. "I grew up in Louisiana and Arkansas," he says. "Down there, everything is fried." But now, weight control and health are more important concerns, so he has learned to modify his cooking techniques to bring down the fat content of his favorite dishes. Hence the unique and tasty way he now prepares the eggplant for a dish that has become a staple around his house—Eggplant Parmesan. "I always liked making Eggplant Parmesan," Brasher says, "but the eggplant soaks up so much oil when you fry it. So I thought up a way of preparing the eggplant without the frying. Now I much prefer eating it this way because it's so much lighter."

Low-Fat Eggplant Parmesan

1. In a large skillet, sauté the garlic, onion, and green pepper in 2 tablespoons olive oil until softened. Add the tomato sauce and tomato paste (or sun-dried tomatoes). Simmer for 30 minutes, stirring occasionally. Add the oregano, basil, cumin, and salt and pepper to taste. Continue cooking over low heat, stirring frequently, for at least 2 hours.

2. Preheat oven to 400 degrees. Peel the eggplants and slice into one-quarter-inch rounds. Lay the eggplant slices on a flat surface and sprinkle with salt. Let drain in a colander for 30 minutes. Wipe the eggplant slices and pat dry with paper towels.

3. Brush the eggplant slices with egg white and coat on both sides with bread crumbs. Bake the slices on a cookie sheet for 10 minutes. Turn and bake for an additional 8 minutes. Both sides should be dark golden brown. Leave oven on at 400 degrees.

4. Brush the bottom of a 10" x 10" baking dish with the remaining 1 teaspoon of olive oil. Make a tight layer of eggplant slices in the bottom of the dish. Top the eggplant with red sauce, then cover with mozzarella cheese. Repeat the layering until all ingredients are used (usually 3 layers). Bake until the sauce and cheese are bubbling, about 15-20 minutes. Cut into squares and serve hot.

- 2 Tbs plus 1 tsp olive oil
- 2 cloves garlic, minced (or more to taste)
- ½ cup onion, chopped
- ½ cup green pepper, chopped
- 3 cans (14½ oz each) tomato sauce
- 1 can (6 oz) tomato paste (or 1 cup chopped sun-dried tomatoes)
- 2 Tbs oregano
- 2 Tbs basil
- 1-2 tsp whole cumin seed (to taste)
- salt and pepper to taste
- 2 medium-large eggplants
- 2 egg whites
- 1-2 cups bread crumbs
- 1 lb mozzarella cheese, sliced or shredded

 EXTRA POINT: Use any leftover red sauce for a pasta side dish to serve with the Eggplant Parmesan. Accompanied with a simple green salad tossed with an oil and balsamic vinegar dressing, this makes a satisfying meal.

Rodney Hampton

RUNNING BACK, NEW YORK GIANTS

Rodney Hampton is the New York Giants' all-time leading rusher with 6,816 yards (entering the 1997 season). And he amassed that total in only seven seasons (1990-96) after being drafted in the first round by New York. The former All-America from Georgia had one of his best seasons in 1995, when he rushed for 1,182 yards and scored 10 touchdowns.

When Hampton moved to New York in 1990, he found he missed the food he ate back home in Houston. "I just don't find the kind of seasonings in New York that I'm accustomed to," he says. "So I called my mother to get cooking instructions from her. I always had watched her cook, but never got in the kitchen and actually did it myself. Now I can go into the kitchen, look around in the cabinets, and make something out of nothing." Hampton says he considers himself the "worst" cook in a family of good cooks, but, he adds, "My friends and teammates seem to like my cooking."

- 1 chicken, cut up
- 1-2 Tbs black pepper, or to taste
- 1-2 Tbs seasoned salt, or to taste
- 1 green onion, chopped
- 1 white onion, chopped
- 1 green bell pepper, chopped
- ½-1 cup of your favorite barbecue sauce

Baked Chicken

1. Preheat oven to 350 degrees. Place the chicken pieces in a large baking pan. Rub chicken with the pepper and seasoned salt.

2. Put the chopped onions and peppers on top of the chicken pieces, and bake for 30 minutes.

3. Pour barbecue sauce evenly over the chicken. Bake for another 20 minutes.

Dave Wannstedt

HEAD COACH, CHICAGO BEARS

Dave Wannstedt began his NFL head-coaching career in Chicago in 1993. In his first four seasons, the Bears had a 32-32 record, reaching the playoffs in 1994. Before taking over in Chicago, Wannstedt was the defensive coordinator for the Super Bowl XXVII-champion Dallas Cowboys. Wannstedt played tackle at the University of Pittsburgh (1970-73) and was drafted in 1974 by the Green Bay Packers, but was injured and never played in the NFL.

Beef Flautas

- ½-1 cup vegetable oil
- 12 flour tortillas
- 1½ lbs lean stew beef
- 1 Tbs salt
- 2 cups water
- 1 pint sour cream
- ¾ cup green onions, chopped
- 1 cup Monterey jack cheese, shredded
- salt and pepper to taste
- ½-1 cup canned green chilies, diced
- guacamole

1. Heat the oil, about one-quarter inch deep, in a frying pan. Fry the tortillas, one at a time, for 15-20 seconds on each side. Remove and cool until they can be handled easily, then roll each tortilla into a tube. Place seam side down, allow the oil to drain, and cool completely.

2. Place the water in a large pot, and add the salt. Drop in the beef and bring to a boil. Turn down the heat and simmer the beef for 1 hour. Drain, cool, and shred the beef.

3. Mix together two-thirds of the sour cream, and all the green onions, Monterey jack cheese, salt, and pepper. Add the shredded beef and mix well.

4. Preheat oven to 350 degrees.

5. Stuff the beef mixture into the tortilla tubes and place in a single layer in a baking dish. Sprinkle with the green chilies.

6. Bake for 20 minutes. Serve with a guacamole garnish and the remaining sour cream.

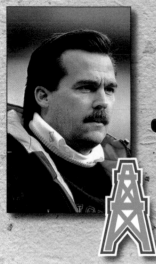

Jeff Fisher

HEAD COACH, TENNESSEE OILERS

At the start of the 1994 NFL season, Jeff Fisher was the Oilers' defensive co-ordinator. With six games remaining, he became the team's head coach. Since then, Fisher has guided the Oilers through a rebuilding process that included an 8-8 record in 1996. Fisher was drafted by Chicago after playing defensive back on USC's 1978 national championship team; he also was a Pacific-10 All-Academic selection. Fisher played cornerback and returned kicks for the Bears from 1981-84. He still holds club season records for punt-return yardage (509 in 1981) and punt returns (58 in 1984).

The Fishers Annual Lobster Party

MENU
- Lobster Tail
- Grilled Lobster Claws
- Barbecued Pork Tenderloin
- Caesar Salad
- Corn on the Cob
- Toasted French Bread

Barbecued Pork Tenderloin

- 2 cloves garlic, finely chopped
- ¼ cup olive oil
- ¼ cup Worcestershire sauce
- ½ cup soy sauce
- ¼ - ½ cup teriyaki sauce
- fresh ground pepper to taste
- 2 pork tenderloins

1. In a medium mixing bowl or large glass measuring cup combine the garlic and olive oil.
2. Add the Worcestershire sauce and stir. Add the soy sauce and teriyaki sauce and mix well. Add fresh ground pepper to taste.
3. Lay the pork tenderloins in a large glass baking dish. Pour the marinade over the tenderloins. Cover and marinate in the refrigerator 1 to 6 hours prior to use.
4. Prepare the barbecue coals. Grill the pork tenderloin over the coals until desired degree of doneness is reached. Slice and serve.

Party Lobsters

1. Bring a large pot of water to a boil. Add the spice mix.

2. Prepare barbecue coals.

3. Boil the lobsters in the water 8-10 minutes. Drain the lobsters and remove
the claws and tails.

4. Put the claws on the outside edges of the grill, where they will not get too
hot. Put the tails briefly over the heat.

5. Clean and split the lobster tails. Serve the tails together with the
claws, accompanied by lemon wedges and melted butter .

- live lobsters
- lobster or crab boil
  spice mix

Dermontti Dawson

CENTER, PITTSBURGH STEELERS

Following in the iron-man tradition of nine-time Pro Bowl center Mike Webster, who preceded him in Pittsburgh, Dawson has joined the ranks of the elite at his position. Through 1996, Dawson had started 132 consecutive games and was the only Steelers player to start every game in that eight-year span (1989-1996). He was named to his fifth consecutive Pro Bowl following the 1996 season.

"This Chicken Parmesan recipe comes from my wife Regina," Dawson says. *"It's a good basic recipe, one that she developed by experimenting in the kitchen. The secret, I think, is that little sprinkle of sugar in the tomato sauce. It keeps the tomato flavor from being too overbearing."* Dawson says he can cook well, as son Brandon, 6, and daughter Briana, 3, can attest. *"But my wife's always teasing me,"* he laughs. *"She says, 'You only cook when I'm not home.'"*

Chicken Parmesan

- 6-8 boneless, skinless chicken breasts
- seasoned salt, to taste
- garlic powder, to taste
- 2 cans (15 oz) Italian-style tomatoes, juice included
- ½ tsp oregano
- ½ tsp basil
- 2 Tbs sugar
- 2 Tbs cornstarch
- ¼ cup Parmesan cheese, grated
- 1½-2 cups mozzarella cheese, shredded

1. Preheat oven to 400 degrees.

2. Trim any visible fat from the chicken. Sprinkle with the seasoned salt and garlic powder. Place in a covered baking dish and bake for 15-20 minutes.

3. While the chicken is baking, mix the tomatoes, oregano, basil, sugar, cornstarch, and Parmesan cheese in a medium saucepan. Cook over medium heat until bubbly, stirring occasionally.

4. Pour the tomato mixture over the chicken. Sprinkle with the mozzarella cheese. Return the chicken to the oven and bake uncovered for 10-15 minutes, or until the cheese is completely melted.

EXTRA POINT: The Dawsons suggest serving this chicken dish with broccoli and a flavored pasta tossed with olive oil and Parmesan cheese.

Regina and Dermontti Dawson

Manu Tuiasosopo

DEFENSIVE TACKLE, SEATTLE SEAHAWKS 1979-1983, SAN FRANCISCO 49ERS 1984-86

Tuiasosopo, Seattle's first-round draft pick in 1979, played five seasons with the Seahawks before joining San Francisco in 1984. In eight NFL seasons, he played every position on the defensive line. Tuiasosopo had a sack for the 49ers in Super Bowl XIX. He also was a starter on UCLA's 1976 Rose Bowl team. His first name, Manu'ula, means "happy bird."

"In the South Pacific, each culture has its own style of pig roast," Tuiasosopo says. "In Samoa, we don't dig the umu *[pit] as deep as in other places. And the Tongans cook their pigs on a rotisserie." Tuiasosopo stages pig roasts on request for schools, churches, and charity events. "It's great for people to gather around the* umu *and experience what it's like when the cooked pig is uncovered," he says. Tuiasosopo has modified the pit-roasting technique for the mainland, where the traditional materials are not available. "Back in the islands," he says, "we use coconut, banana, and breadfruit fronds and leaves to cover the pig instead of newspaper and aluminum foil and tarps."*

MATERIALS

- river rocks the size of a big NFL defensive lineman's fist—enough to layer an area approximately 3' x 4'
- wire netting (chicken wire)—enough to wrap once around the pig
- several medium-size tree stumps and enough firewood to burn up to two hours to heat up the river rocks
- box of cabbage clippings (from the local grocery store)
- 100 yards aluminum foil
- 1 hose
- 4 large buckets
- newspaper, spread out and soaked with water
- canvas tarps, large enough to cover the cooking area
- Serving trays, pans, and large cooking forks (to shred meat)

INGREDIENTS

- 90 lb USDA approved whole pig, completely cleaned and thawed, with legs tucked
- 1 box rock salt
- salt and pepper to taste
- garlic powder to taste
- 5-6 bunches green onions, chopped
- sliced pineapple and parsley for garnish

Kalua Pig Roast PREPARATION

1. You know how to start a charcoal barbecue with briquettes (without using lighter fluid), only now you are starting an *umu* with river rocks instead of coals. Select a flat area of ground away from any flammables, trees, buildings, sprinklers, etc. The cooking area should be approximately 4 to 5 feet square.

2. Dig a pit in the cooking area approximately 6-8 inches deep (or use the length of the shovel blade as a guide to depth), and 2½ x 4 feet square. Reserve the dirt you remove.

3. Place the tree stumps in the middle of the pit. Arrange the firewood around the stumps. Your goal is to have them burn for up to 1½-2 hours.

4. Place the rocks on top of the wood. You should have enough rocks to layer the bottom of the 2½ x 4-foot pit and to build up alongside the pig when the pig has been placed in the *umu*. It's better to have too many rocks than not enough.

5. Start the fire in the pit. The 1½-2-hour heating time is only an estimate. Always rely more on your visual appraisal of the rocks. You want to see a reddish *glow*

over all the rocks—this is key. The black "carbon" you see on the rocks initially will burn off as the heating continues.

6. While the rocks are heating, set up a staging area near the pit (preferably with a sturdy table) for all the ingredients and materials.

7. Spread out the wire netting on the table and lay the pig on its back on top of the wire. Rinse the pig thoroughly with the hose (be sure the runoff doesn't wet the pit). Rub the pig with rock salt so that the salt sticks to its skin.

8. **The next step is very dangerous. Extreme caution should be taken for everyone's safety.** When all the river rocks have heated to a reddish glow, *as quickly as possible* remove all the remaining wood. Set aside an area, beside the *umu* (but away from the staging area) to place the charred wood and stumps.

9. Once you have removed all the wood, use a shovel to pick up one small rock. Blow off any ash or debris and place the rock in the pig's neck. Then put two large rocks in the body cavity of the pig. Wrap the wire netting tightly around the pig, twisting the ends of the wire to hold it in place. Meanwhile, someone should spread the hot rocks around in the pit to create a level layer large enough on which to put the pig.

10. Spread a thin layer of the cabbage clippings over the rocks. Put the pig on its back on top of the cabbage clippings. With one person standing at each side of the *umu*, layer the aluminum foil over the pig, alternating the foil lengthwise and widthwise, covering the cooking pit (three or four layers should be sufficient).

11. Place the wet newspaper over the foil. Wetting the newspaper will expose where the heat is leaking from the pit. Put more newspaper down on top of the foil to cover any leaks. Cover the edges of the pit

well. Layer the newspaper on top and around the edges until all telltale steam leaks disappear.

12. Overlay the pit completely with the tarps.

13. Shovel the dirt from the hole on top of, and around, the tarps. Make absolutely sure no steam is leaking; pay close attention to the edges. The process of "closing the *umu*" should be completed quickly.

14. Depending on the heat of the rocks, and how swiftly you moved to cover the pig completely, the cooking time will be approximately 4-5 hours.

15. While the pig is roasting, clean up around the pit and staging area. Shortly before the cooking is complete, set up the table for serving the Kalua Pig. Prepare the trays, pans, and forks, and put out the salt, pepper, garlic powder, and green onions.

16. When the cooking is complete, remove the dirt from the tarp. Fill the buckets with water. Grab the end of the tarp and pull it all the way back to cover the dirt at the opposite side of the pit. Cool your hands in the water buckets. Peel off all the newspaper and place on top of the tarp at the edge of the pit. Next, carefully peel off the aluminum foil and place on top of the newspaper.

17. **This step is very dangerous and hot—use caution!** Wearing pot holders, grab the pig by the wire netting and carry it to the serving area. Undo the wire netting and fold it back under the pig. The pig should be a golden brown color and the skin should be crusty. Cut the meat to your preference. It is recommended you start with the shoulders and work to the hams.

18. Place the large meat portions in the pans. Shred the meat with the meat forks. Sprinkle the meat with the salt, pepper, garlic powder, and green onions to taste. Place the shredded meat on serving plates and garnish with sliced pineapple and parsley. Enjoy!

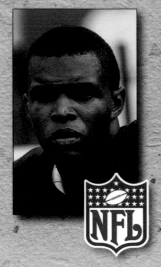

Gale Sayers

RUNNING BACK, CHICAGO BEARS (1965-1971)

Pro Football Hall of Fame running back Sayers combined agility, instinct, strength, and speed to become one of the best players in NFL history. He set an NFL record by scoring 22 touchdowns for the Bears in 1965 and equaled another NFL record that year by scoring 6 touchdowns in one game against San Francisco. He played in four Pro Bowls (1966-68, 1970) and was named outstanding back in three of those games. Sayers led the NFL in rushing in 1966. He came back from a serious knee injury in 1968 to lead the league in rushing again in 1969.

Gale's wife Ardythe is a "scratch cook." "My mother was a professional cook," she explains. "I learned from her to cook without using recipes. She had them all in her head. We used to cook together when I was growing up, and we often baked cookies and pies. She really taught me to improvise." Ardythe says she likes the name of her dish, "Texas Caviar." "It's really just a healthy vegetable dip," she says. "But whenever I serve it at a party, people like it so much they ask me for a bowl and a spoon to eat it as a side dish."

- **2 cans (14 oz each) black-eyed peas, drained**
- **1 can (15 oz) white hominy, drained**
- **2 medium tomatoes, chopped**
- **4 green onions, chopped**
- **2 large cloves garlic, minced**
- **1 medium green bell pepper, seeded and chopped**
- **2 jalapeño peppers, finely chopped**
- **½ cup onion, chopped**
- **½ cup parsley, finely chopped**
- **1 bottle (8 oz) Italian salad dressing**

Texas Caviar

1. In a large bowl, combine the black-eyed peas and hominy.

2. Add the tomatoes, green onions, and garlic. Mix well.

3. Add the green and jalapeño peppers, onion, and parsley. Toss well.

4. Pour the salad dressing over the vegetables and toss gently to coat well. Cover and refrigerate for at least 2 hours.

5. Drain, and serve with tortilla chips.

 EXTRA POINT: This dish is easy to make and can be prepared the night before a party.

Yeast Rolls

- 1 cup boiling water
- 1 cup solid shortening
- 1 cup sugar
- 1 ½ tsp salt
- 2 large eggs, beaten
- 2 packages dry yeast
- 1 cup warm water
- 6 cups all-purpose flour, unsifted

1. In a large mixing bowl, pour the boiling water over the shortening, sugar, and salt. Blend, then let cool.

2. Add the beaten eggs to the mixture. Mix well.

3. Sprinkle the yeast into the cup of warm water. Stir and add to the shortening mixture.

4. Gradually add the flour. Mix well.

5. Put the bowl in the refrigerator and chill for at least 4 hours.

6. Roll out the dough on a floured surface. Brush lightly with vegetable oil and let rise 3 hours before baking.

7. Preheat oven to 400 degrees. Form the dough into desired shapes and bake for 10-15 minutes or until golden brown.

 EXTRA POINT: This dough will keep in the refrigerator for up to two weeks. "I like to make this dough ahead and use it as we need it," Ardythe says. "It also works well cut into small pieces to make party canapés and bite-sized sandwiches."

Ardythe and Gale Sayers.

Steve Young

QUARTERBACK, SAN FRANCISCO 49ERS

Young is second to none among NFL quarterbacks in the 1990s. He has led the NFL in passer rating five of the last six seasons and owns the NFL record for career rating (96.2). Young, a five-time Pro Bowl selection, led San Francisco to victory in Super Bowl XXIX and was named the game's most valuable player. In addition, he earned consensus NFL MVP honors in both 1992 and 1994.

"Steve's cookie sandwich is only for the really brave, and, I must add, is not mother approved," says Sherry Young, Steve's mom. "To make it, take two cookies warm from the oven, and place a tablespoon of raw cookie dough in between them. He claims it is delicious."

- **4 cups all-purpose flour**
- **¾ cup quick oatmeal**
- **2 tsp baking soda**
- **2 tsp salt**
- **2 cups solid shortening**
- **1 ½ cups granulated sugar**
- **1 ½ cups brown sugar, packed**
- **2 tsp vanilla**
- **4 large eggs**
- **4 cups chocolate morsels**
- **1 - 1 ½ cups walnut or pecan pieces (optional)**

Sherry's Chocolate Chip Cookies

1. Preheat oven to 375 degrees.

2. In a large mixing bowl, combine the flour, oatmeal, baking soda, and salt.

3. In another large mixing bowl, beat the shortening, sugars, and vanilla. Add the eggs one at a time, beating well after each addition.

4. Gradually, beat in the flour mixture. Stir in the chocolate morsels and optional nuts.

5. Drop the cookie dough by rounded tablespoon onto ungreased baking sheets. Bake for 9-11 minutes, or until golden brown. Remove the cookies from the oven and let stand for two minutes. Move the cookies to wire racks to cool completely. (Makes about 10 dozen cookies.)

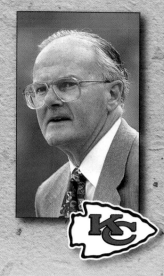

Lamar Hunt

OWNER, KANSAS CITY CHIEFS

Hunt was the founder of the American Football League and the Kansas City Chiefs (who began play as the Dallas Texans in 1960). The Chiefs played in the first Super Bowl and they won Super Bowl IV, the last game played before the AFL and NFL merged into one league. Hunt is credited with coming up with the name "Super Bowl," which was suggested by his daughter's favorite toy, a super ball. In 1972, Hunt became the first AFL personality to be enshrined in the Pro Football Hall of Fame. The AFC Championship Trophy is named in his honor.

Hunt named this colorful cake after the recipe's originator, a Mrs. Jones, who used to make the cake for Hunt every year on his birthday.

CAKE:
- 1 package white cake mix
- 1 package strawberry gelatin
- ½ cup vegetable oil
- ½ cup water
- 4 eggs
- ½ cup sliced frozen strawberries, thawed

ICING:
- 1 stick butter
- 1 box (16 oz) powdered sugar
- ½ cup sliced frozen strawberries, thawed

Jonesey's Strawberry Cake

1. Preheat oven to 325 degrees.

2. In a large mixing bowl, beat the cake mix, gelatin, oil, and water. Add the eggs one at a time, beating after each addition.

3. Drain the strawberries, reserving the juice. Measure one-half cup of strawberries, reserving the rest, and add to the cake batter. Mix well.

4. Pour the batter into a 13" x 9"x 2¼" baking pan. Bake until lightly brown, about 20 minutes. Cool before icing.

5. To make the icing, cream together the butter and powdered sugar. Add one-half cup of strawberries and mix well. Add a little of the reserved strawberry juice as needed to maintain the consistency of the icing.

 EXTRA POINT: This sweet cake's pink color makes it ideal for children's birthday celebrations.

Lindy Infante

HEAD COACH, INDIANAPOLIS COLTS

Infante began his second stint as an NFL head coach in 1996 by taking the Colts to a second consecutive playoff appearance. Infante previously was the head coach in Green Bay (1988-1991), and was named NFL coach of the year in 1989, when the Packers finished 10-6. Infante, a running back at the University of Florida, was an eleventh-round draft choice by the Buffalo Bills of the American Football League in 1963.

"The thing that I like best about this recipe—besides the fact that it tastes great— is that it is so easy," says Stephanie Infante, Lindy's wife. "But it looks like you've spent a long time on dessert."

Crunchy Coffee Frozen Torte

1. Combine the water and coffee crystals in a measuring cup. Set aside.
2. Place the frozen yogurt in a medium bowl. Let it soften until the yogurt can be smoothly stirred. Add the coffee and chopped cookies. Mix well.
3. Spoon the mixture evenly into an 8-inch springform pan. Freeze 4 hours, or until firm. Cut into wedges and garnish with nonfat whipped topping, maraschino cherries, and fresh mint.

- ¼ cup hot water
- 2 Tbs instant coffee crystals
- 2 pints vanilla nonfat frozen yogurt or low-fat ice cream
- 8 chocolate cookies, coarsely chopped
- garnishes: nonfat whipped topping, maraschino cherries, fresh mint

 EXTRA POINT: This recipe also is delicious topped with chopped fresh fruit or berries.

Teams of the National

AFC EAST

Buffalo Bills

Indianapolis Colts

Miami Dolphins

**New England
Patriots**

New York Jets

AFC CENTRAL

Baltimore Ravens

Cincinnati Bengals

**Jacksonville
Jaguars**

Pittsburgh Steelers

Tennessee Oilers

AFC WEST

Denver Broncos

Kansas City Chiefs

Oakland Raiders

**San Diego
Chargers**

Seattle Seahawks

Football League

NFC EAST	NFC CENTRAL	NFC WEST

Arizona Cardinals

Chicago Bears

Atlanta Falcons

Dallas Cowboys

Detroit Lions

Carolina Panthers

New York Giants

Green Bay Packers

New Orleans Saints

Philadelphia Eagles

Minnesota Vikings

St. Louis Rams

**Washington
Redskins**

**Tampa Bay
Buccaneers**

**San Francisco
49ers**

PRESEASON

Lou Groza
- Cheese Loaf
- Blueberry Spinach Salad

Joe Phillips
- Salsa Pico de Gallo
- Pasta With Sun-Dried Tomatoes and Greens

Chris Berman
- Baby Back, Back, Back Ribs

Mike Ditka
- Broccoli and Macaroni Hollandaise
- Diana's Creamy Coleslaw

Tony Dungy
- Tony's Shrimp Gumbo

Sean Jones
- Jamaican Jerk Chicken

Cody Risien
- Blushing Bunnies
- Texas Sheet Cake

Junior Seau
- Barbecued Salmon Salad With Sun-Dried Tomato Vinaigrette

- Grilled Mahi-Mahi With Spicy Pineapple Relish

Rich Gannon
- Chicken Salsa Chili

Paul Tagliabue
- Summer Risotto

Johnnie Morton
- Johnnie's Drumettes
- Peanut Butter Cup Pie

Marty Schottenheimer
- After-the-Game Beef Stew
- Tailgate Corn Salad
- Lemon Squares

Tom Flores
- Dijon Chicken With Gorgonzola
- Marinated Flank Steak

Tim Bream
- Crunchy Chocolate Chip Cookies

Jack Kemp
- Moist Chocolate Cake

Baby Back, Back, Back Ribs; Johnnie's Drumettes; Tailgate Corn Salad

Lou Groza

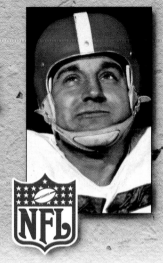

TACKLE/KICKER, CLEVELAND BROWNS (1950-59, 1961-67)

Pro Football Hall of Fame enshrinee Groza played for 21 seasons with the Browns—four years in the All-America Football Conference and 17 in the NFL. As a kicker, Groza scored 1,608 points in his professional career; as a tackle, he was named all-pro six times. His 16-yard, last-minute field goal helped the Browns defeat the Los Angeles Rams for the 1950 NFL championship. In 1954, Groza was named NFL player of the year for his part in leading the Browns to their second NFL title.

When asked if she enjoys cooking, Jackie Groza says, "We've been married forty-seven years. I've done a lot of it." Jackie says that a meal of Blueberry Spinach Salad and Cheese Loaf is one of Lou's favorites. "It makes for a nice luncheon or light supper."

Cheese Loaf

1. Preheat oven to 350 degrees.
2. In a mixing bowl, combine all ingredients except the bread. Blend well.
3. Slice the bread at 1½-inch intervals, but do not cut all the way through the loaf—stop each cut about one-fourth inch from the bottom of the loaf. Spread the cheese mixture in between each slice.
4. Wrap the loaf in foil and heat for 6 to 8 minutes in the oven. Remove from the oven, fold back the foil to expose the top of the loaf, and return to the oven for 2 to 3 minutes more.

- 1 cup mozzarella cheese, shredded
- 2 Tbs butter or margarine, softened
- ½ tsp garlic salt
- 4 medium green onions, chopped
- 1 package (3 oz) cream cheese
- 1 loaf unsliced French bread

Blueberry Spinach Salad

SALAD:
- ½ lb fresh spinach
- ½ lb Bibb lettuce
- 1 cup fresh blueberries
- 4 oz bleu cheese, crumbled
- ½ cup pecans, toasted
- red raspberries to garnish

DRESSING:
- ½ cup vegetable oil
- 3 Tbs white wine vinegar
- 1 tsp dijon mustard
- 1 tsp sugar
- salt to taste

1. Thoroughly clean the spinach. Wash the lettuce. Pat both dry, then tear into bite-size pieces.
2. Put the spinach and lettuce pieces in a large salad bowl. Add the blueberries and bleu cheese.
3. Make the dressing by combining all dressing ingredients in a small bowl or glass measuring cup. Whisk to blend.
4. Pour the dressing over the salad and toss well. Sprinkle pecans over the salad, then garnish with the blueberries.

EXTRA POINT: Jackie Groza says you can use other kinds of nuts on the salad, but pecans work best for her taste.

Joe Phillips

DEFENSIVE TACKLE, KANSAS CITY CHIEFS

Joe Phillips has been a force on the Chiefs' defensive line since coming to Kansas City as a free agent from San Diego in 1992. Phillips started every game in 1996 for the fourth consecutive season. Originally a draft choice by Minnesota in 1986, Phillips played one season with the Vikings before joining the Chargers.

Cynthia and Joe Phillips were in law school when they began taking a serious interest in cooking. "On the weekends when we weren't studying," Cynthia says, "we used cooking as a way to get away without really getting away." Cynthia and Joe met on the beach in Hawaii, where Cynthia was acting in an episode of Magnum PI *and Joe was there for the Aloha Bowl with Southern Methodist University. Joe, who now practices real estate and contract law in the offseason, is fond of pasta, and "carbo loads" with it before games. Cynthia, another pasta lover, has passed the bar in three states, and somehow still finds time for her acting and her television talk show in Kansas City,* Tailgate Special, *which airs prior to Chiefs home games.*

Salsa Pico De Gallo

1. In a bowl, combine all of the ingredients at right. Mix well and refrigerate for two hours.
2. Serve chilled with tortilla chips.

- 3 tomatoes, diced
- 2 bunches scallions, finely chopped
- 2 cucumbers, peeled, seeded, and diced
- 3 green peppers, roasted, peeled, and diced
- ½ bunch cilantro, finely chopped
- 1 Tbs horseradish
- 3 jalapeño peppers, minced
- juice of 2 limes
- 2 Tbs salt
- 2 Tbs white pepper

- 1 whole bulb of garlic, peeled and finely chopped
- 10 sun-dried tomatoes, chopped
- ¾-1 cup olive oil (or to taste)
- 1½ cups spinach or fresh greens, chopped
- 1 lb spaghettini or cappellini

Pasta With Sun-Dried Tomatoes and Greens

1. In a large skillet sauté the garlic and sun-dried tomatoes in olive oil. Add the spinach or greens and cook until wilted.
2. Cook the pasta in boiling water following package directions until *al dente*. Drain.
3. Toss the pasta with the sauce and serve immediately.

 EXTRA POINT: The salsa also can be heated and served as an accompaniment to grilled fish, such as ahi, halibut, or swordfish.

Chris Berman

SPORTSCASTER, ESPN

Berman has become one of America's most popular sports anchormen since his arrival at ESPN in 1979. He is the central figure in ESPN's NFL studio programming, as host for *NFL Countdown*, *NFL Prime Time*, and ESPN's NFL draft coverage, among other shows. Noted for his humor and enthusiasm, Berman's trademark use of off-the-wall player nicknames while narrating highlights has made him a favorite with NFL fans. In 1996, Berman joined ABC's *Monday Night Football* as halftime host.

Bar-B-Chris Berman plays in the backyard.

"Every summer, my family and I go out to Sun Valley, Idaho, to visit my brother and his family," Berman says. "My sister-in-law Kate is a fantastic cook and makes these ribs whenever I'm in town. What better way to enjoy the Wild West!"

- **6 lbs baby back pork ribs**
- **2 cups water**
  SAUCE:
- **4 cups tomato ketchup (32 oz bottle)**
- **⅓ cup onion, finely chopped**
- **¼ cup brown sugar**
- **3 Tbs lemon juice**
- **3 Tbs rum**
- **3 Tbs Worcestershire sauce**
- **2 Tbs liquid hickory flavoring**
- **2 tsp Louisiana pepper sauce**

Baby Back, Back, Back Ribs

1. Preheat oven to 350 degrees.

2. Cut the rib slabs in half, leaving 6-8 ribs per section. In a large roasting pan, arrange the ribs evenly, then add the water. Cover pan tightly with a lid or foil to prevent steam from escaping. Bake for 3 hours.

3. About 2 hours into the baking time, make the sauce. In a large saucepan, combine all the sauce ingredients. Simmer over low heat for 1 hour, stirring occasionally.

4. Prepare the coals in a barbecue. Remove the ribs from the roasting pan. Discard the water.

5. Cover the ribs with sauce, saving about 1½ cups of the sauce for later use at the table. Grill the ribs on the barbecue for about 5 minutes per side, or until slightly charred. Serve with the reserved sauce.

Mike Ditka

HEAD COACH, NEW ORLEANS SAINTS

After four seasons with NBC television as an NFL analyst, Mike Ditka returns to the sidelines in 1997 to lead the Saints. Ditka previously was head coach of the Chicago Bears for 11 seasons, compiling a 112-68 record, including a victory in Super Bowl XX. The former tight end played 12 seasons in the NFL with Chicago, Philadelphia, and Dallas (he caught a touchdown pass in the Cowboys' victory in Super Bowl VI). Ditka, one of the two men to win Super Bowls as a player, assistant coach, and head coach, was inducted into the Pro Football Hall of Fame in 1988. He is the owner of Iron Mike's, a restaurant in Chicago.

- 3 Tbs butter
- 3 Tbs flour
- 1 ½ tsp salt
- ⅛ tsp pepper
- 1 ½ cups milk
- ¾ cup mayonnaise
- 1 package (7 oz) artichoke macaroni shells
- 2 cups cooked broccoli, chopped
- 1 cup cheddar cheese, grated

Broccoli and Macaroni Hollandaise

1. Preheat oven to 350 degrees.

2. In a medium saucepan, melt the butter. Stir in the flour, salt, and pepper. Gradually add the milk and cook, stirring constantly, until thickened. Fold in the mayonnaise.

3. Cook the macaroni in boiling salted water until tender. Drain and rinse, then drain again.

4. In a greased one-and-a-half quart casserole, place layers of the macaroni, broccoli, and white sauce, ending with a layer of sauce. Sprinkle with the cheddar cheese.

5. Bake for 20 minutes and serve hot.

Mike Ditka enjoys a quick bite at Iron Mike's.

Diana's Creamy Coleslaw

1. In a large mixing bowl, combine the cabbage and the onion.

2. In another mixing bowl or large measuring cup, blend the mayonnaise, sugar, vinegar, salt, and celery seed.

3. Pour the dressing over the cabbage and onion mixture and toss well. Place the coleslaw in a serving bowl and top with optional green pepper garnish.

- **3 cups cabbage, shredded**
- **⅓ cup onion, finely chopped**
- **½ cup mayonnaise or salad dressing**
- **1 Tbs sugar**
- **1 Tbs vinegar**
- **½ tsp salt**
- **½ tsp celery seed**
- **1 small green bell pepper, sliced into thin rings for garnish (optional)**

Tony Dungy

HEAD COACH, TAMPA BAY BUCCANEERS

Tony Dungy was named Tampa Bay's head coach in 1996 after serving 15 seasons as an NFL assistant with Pittsburgh, Kansas City, and Minnesota. In his first season, the Buccaneers rallied from a 1-8 start to win five of their last seven games. A former quarterback at the University of Minnesota, Dungy played safety in the NFL for Pittsburgh (1977-78) and the San Francisco 49ers (1979). He became the NFL's youngest assistant in 1981, when he was hired to coach defensive backs by the Steelers at age 25.

- 3 Tbs vegetable oil
- 1 ½ tsp all-purpose flour
- 1 lb fresh shrimp, shelled and deveined
- 1 cup celery, chopped
- 2 medium onions, chopped
- 1 ½ lbs fresh okra, sliced into quarter-inch rounds
- 1 can (14 ½ oz) tomatoes
- 4 cups water
- 2 bay leaves
- salt and pepper to taste
- 1 can (6 oz) tomato paste
- ½ lb lobster meat, cooked
- hot cooked rice

Tony's Shrimp Gumbo

1. In a medium skillet, heat 2 tablespoons of oil over medium-high heat. Make a roux by gradually stirring in the flour. Stir constantly until the mixture turns a rich, dark brown. (Do not allow the flour to burn.) Stir in the shrimp. Cook 5 minutes and set aside.

2. In a large saucepan, heat the remaining tablespoon of oil over medium heat. Add the celery and onions and cook until they become soft. Add the okra. Cook until the okra ceases to rope (about 30 minutes).

3. When the okra is done, add the tomatoes and their liquid, water, bay leaves, and the salt and pepper. Stir in the shrimp mixture. Add the tomato paste after about 1 minute and stir. Cover and simmer for 30 minutes.

4. Add the lobster meat and stir. Turn off heat. Remove the bay leaves.

5. Serve the gumbo over rice in flat-bottomed bowls.

Lauren and Tony Dungy

Sean Jones

DEFENSIVE END, GREEN BAY PACKERS

Sean Jones traded his helmet for a TNT Sports microphone following the 1996 season. But he ended his 13-year NFL career in style—with the Green Bay Packers' 35-21 victory over New England in Super Bowl XXXI. Jones broke into the league in 1984 with the Raiders, playing four seasons in Los Angeles before joining the Houston Oilers. He signed with Green Bay as an unrestricted free agent in 1994. Jones retired in ninth place on the all-time NFL sack list with 113 career sacks.

"Most recipes in Jamaica are 'a pinch of this and a pinch of that,'" says former NFL defensive end Jones, who was born in Kingston. "This is a family recipe, but everyone it has been passed down to makes it their own way. These measures are as exact as I can make them, but it is a matter of touch and taste. Just be sure to watch the salt and make it spicy, but not too hot."

- 1 chicken, cut up
  CHICKEN SEASONING:
- ¼ tsp each: salt, black pepper, white pepper, garlic powder, onion powder, cloves (whole or ground), pimentoes, oregano, thyme, basil, paprika
- 3 fresh Scotch Bonnet (habañero) peppers, finely diced (separated into two equal portions)
  MARINADE:
- 4 green onions, chopped
- 1 large onion, finely chopped
- 2 cloves garlic, finely chopped
- Scotch Bonnet peppers, diced
- 1-3 Tbs soy sauce
- ¼ bottle Jamaican jerk paste (available in ethnic and specialty markets)
- 1-2 bottles beer

Jamaican Jerk Chicken

1. Cut the chicken pieces in half with a cleaver.
2. Combine the chicken seasoning ingredients. Knead the mixture into the chicken pieces then place them in a large bowl or dish. Cover and refrigerate for at least 1 hour.
3. Remove the kneaded chicken to a plate. In the bowl the chicken was in, combine the marinade ingredients. Be careful not to make the marinade too thin, so add the beer gradually.
4. Place the chicken back in the bowl with the marinade and stir to coat well. Refrigerate overnight.
5. Prepare the barbecue coals. Wrap the chicken pieces in a packet made from 3 layers of *heavy-duty* aluminum foil. Reserve the marinade.
6. Place the foil packet of chicken on the grate and cook 1 hour. Carefully open the packet and baste the chicken well with marinade. Reseal the packet and cook another hour; baste again, and so on each hour. The process takes a total of 4 hours. Remove the chicken from the foil packet and serve.

 EXTRA POINT: The small orange Scotch Bonnet peppers are extremely hot. Many cooks wear rubber gloves when handling chiles. If you don't, be sure to wash your hands well with soap afterward to remove the chile oil before touching any sensitive skin.

Cody Risien

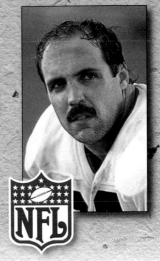

TACKLE, CLEVELAND BROWNS (1979-1983,1985-89)

Risien, a seventh-round draft pick in 1979, developed into a star at right tackle for the Cleveland Browns. He played five seasons, then suffered a knee injury that sidelined him in 1984. Risien returned to form in 1985 and was named to consecutive Pro Bowls in 1986-87. Risien played college football at Texas A&M.

"Everyone enjoys a treat from the Lone Star state." Risien says. "My wife Kathy and I both grew up in Texas. Even though we now live in Cleveland, we still like to serve this Texas Sheet Cake." And as for the Blushing Bunnies? Risien says it's very popular with his three daughters, whom he calls his "Risienettes." "It's a recipe from my childhood," Cody says. "Make it and you'll understand the name."

Blushing Bunnies

1. In a medium saucepan, melt the butter. Add the cheese and heat until melted.

2. Add the tomato soup and stir. Add the mustard and blend well.

3. Serve in bowls over saltine crackers or corn chips.

- 1 Tbs butter or margarine
- 1 cup cheddar cheese, shredded
- 1 can (10¾ oz) tomato soup
- ¼ tsp dry mustard

CAKE:
- 2 cups sugar
- 2 cups all-purpose flour
- 2 sticks butter or margarine
- 2 Tbs cocoa
- 1 cup water
- ½ cup buttermilk
- 2 eggs
- 1 tsp vanilla
- 1 tsp baking soda

ICING:
- 1 stick butter or margarine
- 4 Tbs cocoa
- 6 Tbs milk
- 1 box (16 oz) powdered sugar
- 1 tsp vanilla
- 1 cup pecans (Texas pecans are best)

Texas Sheet Cake

1. Preheat oven to 400 degrees.

2. In a large mixing bowl, combine the sugar and flour.

3. In a small saucepan, melt the butter or margarine. Add the cocoa and stir. Add the water and bring to a boil. Pour into the flour mixture and stir.

4. Add the buttermilk to the bowl and mix well. Beat in the eggs, vanilla, and baking soda.

5. Pour the batter into a greased 9" x 13" baking pan. Bake 20 minutes.

6. To make the icing, melt the butter or margarine in a medium saucepan. Add the cocoa and the milk, and heat, stirring, to combine.

7. Remove the pan from the heat. Add the powdered sugar, vanilla, and pecans and blend thoroughly. Ice the cake while it still is warm.

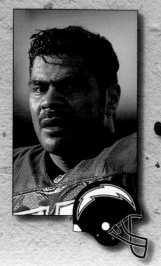

Junior Seau

LINEBACKER, SAN DIEGO CHARGERS

Seau is one of the most electrifying players in the NFL, bringing to the football field an amazing combination of speed, strength, and desire. The San Diego native was voted to his sixth consecutive Pro Bowl in 1996, and has led the Chargers in tackles for the last six seasons. Seau, an All-America selection at Southern California after recording 19 sacks in 1989, was the Chargers' first-round selection in the 1990 NFL draft.

Junior Seau's new restaurant in San Diego is "within punting distance of Qualcomm Stadium." "And it's almost as big," says Kathy Murray, manager of Seau's the Restaurant. "We have 15,000 square feet, including a cigar lounge and a walk-through tunnel that gives people the feeling of entering a stadium." Opened on July 4, 1996, Seau's was named the "Sports Restaurant of the Year" in its rookie season by the San Diego Restaurant Association. "Our recipes were developed in conjunction with a consulting chef," says Murray. "They're a step up from traditional sports-bar fare. But we have great potato skins and chicken wings, too."

Barbecued Salmon Salad With Sun-Dried Tomato Vinaigrette

DRESSING:
- 1 oz sun-dried tomatoes (about 2 Tbs)
- 2 medium cloves garlic, or to taste
- 6 fresh basil leaves
- 4 Tbs balsamic vinegar
- 1 cup olive oil
- salt and pepper to taste

SALAD:
- 1 lb mixed baby field greens (or mixed lettuces), washed and dried
- 2 oz pine nuts, toasted
- 4 small salmon steaks (approximately 3 oz each) grilled over barbecue or blackened in a cast-iron pan
- 1 large ripe tomato cut into 8 wedges

1. In a blender or food processor, combine the sun-dried tomatoes, garlic, basil, and balsamic vinegar. Purée until smooth.

2. Slowly add the olive oil until it incorporates into the dressing. Season with salt and pepper to taste.

3. In a mixing bowl, toss the greens with the sun-dried tomato dressing.

4. Divide the greens onto 4 chilled salad plates. Sprinkle the toasted pine nuts over each portion.

5. Flake the blackened salmon with a fork and place the equivalent of one steak on top of each portion. Garnish each plate with two tomato wedges and serve.

- 6-8 pieces of mahi-mahi (approximately 8 oz each) per person
RELISH:
- ¼ of a fresh pineapple, cut into small cubes
- 2 tomatoes, finely diced
- ½ yellow bell pepper, finely diced
- ½ red bell pepper, finely diced
- ½ small yellow onion, diced
- 2-3 jalapeño peppers, minced, to taste
- 2 Tbs fresh cilantro, chopped
- salt and pepper to taste

Grilled Mahi-Mahi With Spicy Pineapple Relish

1. In a large mixing bowl, combine all the relish ingredients and toss to mix well.

2. Grill the mahi-mahi portions.

3. Serve the mahi-mahi on individual plates. Place a rounded tablespoon of the relish on top of the fish so that the relish spreads over the sides of each fish portion.

Rich Gannon

QUARTERBACK, KANSAS CITY CHIEFS

Gannon gives the Chiefs a valuable combination of talent and experience at quarterback. He was drafted in the fourth round in 1987 by New England, then went to Minnesota in a trade prior to the opening of the season. Gannon played six seasons for the Vikings, passing for more than 6,000 yards and 40 touchdowns. He spent one season in Washington before joining the Chiefs as a free agent in 1995.

Chicken Salsa Chili

1. In a large pot, boil the chicken breasts until tender (about 20 minutes). Drain. When cool enough to handle, shred the chicken.

2. In a Dutch oven, mix the chicken with the three types of beans, tomatoes, and salsa. Season to taste with the chili powder.

3. Simmer chili for one hour. Top with shredded cheese, sour cream, and green onions. Serve with tortilla chips.

- 1 lb chicken breast, boneless and skinless
- 1 can (10 oz) garbanzo beans
- 1 can (15 oz) spicy black beans
- 1 can (15 oz) chili beans
- 1 can (15 oz) Mexican-style stewed tomatoes
- ¾ cup of your favorite salsa
- chili powder, sweet or hot, to taste
  TOPPINGS:
- shredded cheese
- sour cream
- chopped green onions

Paul Tagliabue

NFL COMMISSIONER

Tagliabue has represented the NFL for more than a quarter-century. He became NFL Commissioner on November 5, 1989, and has been responsible for maintaining labor peace and overseeing the growth of the sport domestically and internationally. Prior to taking office, he served as the league's principal counsel on important NFL issues including television, expansion, and legislative affairs. Tagliabue originally is from New Jersey. He attended Georgetown University on a basketball scholarship.

As most Italian cooks know, risotto can be a wonderful first course, or it can be a meal in itself. It involves a uniquely Italian way of preparing rice. "My parents made risotto the same way as their parents," says NFL Commissioner Paul Tagliabue, "and the two branches of the family were from different parts of Italy, Genoa and Como. The method for making risotto is universal. Once you have the technique, you can vary the recipe to include any featured ingredient, such as meat, fish, shellfish, mushrooms, or vegetables. The rice and cheese should be authentic for the best flavor, imported if at all possible." Making risotto takes patience and a certain "touch," but it is so good, it is worth all the stirring. "Correct heat is the secret to making good risotto," Tagliabue says. "It should be lively, but not so high that you cannot keep a good balance of broth and creamy consistency as the risotto cooks. If the liquid evaporates too rapidly, the rice cannot cook evenly. If you are using Italian rice, the risotto will cook in twenty-five to thirty minutes."

Summer Risotto

- 1 medium zucchini, sliced into thin rounds
- 1 medium yellow squash, sliced into thin rounds
- 8 cups chicken broth (regular or low fat)
- 1 medium white onion, finely chopped
- 3 Tbs butter
- 2 Tbs vegetable oil
- salt (a pinch, or to taste)
- 2 cups Arborio rice
- salt and freshly ground black pepper to taste
- ½ cup grated Parmesan cheese (preferably Parmigiano-Reggiano)
- ½ cup chives, finely chopped

1. Steam the zucchini and squash for 5 minutes. Set aside. Put the broth in a saucepan and simmer.

2. In a heavy skillet that distributes heat evenly, sauté the onion in 2 tablespoons of the butter and the 2 tablespoons of oil. Add a pinch of salt, and cook until the onion is soft and almost beginning to brown.

3. Add the rice and sauté for 1-2 minutes, stirring well to coat the rice in the butter and oil.

4. Add 1 cup of the simmering broth to the rice and stir while cooking, until the rice absorbs the liquid. When the rice dries out, add another half cup of broth and continue to stir and cook. Repeat this process, adding broth and stirring, for the entire 25-30 minutes of cooking time, making certain that the rice does not stick to the bottom of the skillet. Add liquid as the rice dries out, but don't "drown" the rice. If you run out of broth, use water.

*Paul and Chan
Tagliabue*

5. After 10-12 minutes of cooking the risotto, add the zucchini and squash. Continue stirring and adding broth as needed. As the rice finishes cooking, do not swamp it with excess broth or water. The risotto is done when the rice is creamy and tender, but firm to the bite.

6. Turn off the stove. Add the final tablespoon of butter, the salt (if needed) and black pepper, and the Parmesan cheese. Sprinkle the chives over the risotto before you bring it to the table in either a large bowl or in individual servings.

 EXTRA POINT: Risotto is made with special Italian rices, Arborio being the most readily available in America. Look for it in specialty supermarkets or Italian delicatessens.

79

Johnnie Morton

WIDE RECEIVER, DETROIT LIONS

Morton is developing into a full-time offensive threat for the Lions. In 1996, he caught a career-high 55 passes for 714 yards and 6 touchdowns. Morton, an All-America at USC, set a Pacific 10 Conference career record with 3,201 yards receiving. Detroit made him its first-round draft pick in 1994.

- 1 egg, beaten
- 2 cups milk
- 2 cups all-purpose flour
- 3-4 Tbs salt
- 4 tsp black pepper
- 1 tsp monosodium glutamate (optional)
- 3 lbs chicken drumettes
- 2-3 cups vegetable oil

Johnnie's Drumettes

1. Combine the egg and milk.

2. In a bowl, mix the flour, salt, pepper, and the optional msg .

3. Dip the drumettes in the egg-milk mixture, then coat each well with the seasoned flour.

4. In a large skillet (preferably cast iron), fry the drumettes in 2-3 cups oil until golden brown and crispy. Drain on paper towels or brown paper.

 EXTRA POINT: The drumettes also may be cooked in a pressure cooker as you would any fried chicken.

Peanut Butter Cup Pie

1. Preheat oven to 425 degrees.

2. In a large mixing bowl, cream together the butter and the sugar.

3. Add the vanilla and the eggs and blend well.

4. Gradually add the flour and mix well, then blend in the melted peanut butter morsels.

5. Pour the pie filling into the crust. Bake pie at 425 degrees for 5 minutes. Reduce the oven temperature to 350 and bake for an additional 20 minutes. Cool before serving.

- ½ stick (4 Tbs) salted butter, softened
- ½-1 cup sugar (to taste)
- 1 tsp vanilla
- 3 eggs, beaten
- ½ cup all-purpose flour
- ½ lb (8 oz) peanut butter morsels, melted
- 1 chocolate cookie pie crust

Marty Schottenheimer

HEAD COACH, KANSAS CITY CHIEFS

In 12 full seasons as a head coach with Cleveland and Kansas City, Schottenheimer's teams never have had a losing season and have been to the playoffs 10 times. Since taking over at Kansas City in 1989, his Chiefs have won AFC West titles in 1993 and 1995, and made postseason appearances six times in seven seasons (1990-1996). Schottenheimer was an All-America linebacker at the University of Pittsburgh (1962-64). He was drafted by Buffalo, playing four seasons with the Bills (1965-68) and two with the Patriots (1969-1970).

Pat Schottenheimer, Marty's wife, likes to plan ahead. "The thing I like about this beef stew recipe," she says, "is that you can put it in the oven when you leave for the game. It's ready when you get home to celebrate the victory." She also adds that the Lemon Square recipe is "one of Marty's all-time favorites."

- 3 cups (24 oz) tomato-vegetable juice
- 1 tsp sugar
- 6 Tbs minute tapioca
- 1 tsp salt
- black pepper to taste
- 2 lbs steak, cubed
- 3 stalks celery, diced
- 5-6 potatoes, peeled and diced
- 1 large onion, chopped
- 4 carrots, diced

After-the-Game Beef Stew

1. Preheat oven to 250 degrees.
2. In a large mixing bowl, combine the vegetable juice, sugar, tapioca, salt, and pepper.
3. Put the steak and chopped vegetables into a Dutch oven or crock pot. Pour the vegetable juice mixture over all.
4. Cover and bake the stew in the oven, or cook in the crock pot, for 5 hours.

 EXTRA POINT: This stew also can be made the night before and refrigerated. Serve it warm with sourdough bread.

Tailgate Corn Salad

1. Combine all the ingredients in a medium mixing bowl. Stir together gently to coat with liquid.
2. Cover and chill overnight.

- 1 can (12 oz) whole kernel corn
- 1 small onion, chopped
- ½ cup red or green bell pepper, chopped
- 2 Tbs fresh parsley, minced
- 2 Tbs cider vinegar
- 2 Tbs vegetable oil
- ¼ tsp salt
- ¼ tsp pepper

Lemon Squares

1. Preheat oven to 350 degrees.
2. In a large mixing bowl, cream together the butter or margarine and sugar. Gradually add the 1½ cups of flour and mix until the mixture becomes pastry-like.
3. Press the dough into a 9" x 13" baking pan. Bake for 20 minutes.
4. Mix the eggs and sugar. Add the remaining flour, then the lemon juice. Mix well.
5. Pour the lemon mixture over the hot pastry crust. Return to the oven for another 20-25 minutes. Cool and cut into squares.

- ¾ cup butter or margarine
- ½ cup powdered sugar
- 1 ½ cups flour
- 3 eggs
- 1 ½ cups granulated sugar
- 3 Tbs flour
- 4 Tbs lemon juice

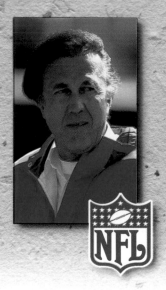

Tom Flores

HEAD COACH, OAKLAND/L.A. RAIDERS 1979-1987, SEATTLE SEAHAWKS 1992-94

Flores is one of only two men in NFL history (New Orleans Saints head coach Mike Ditka is the other) to win a Super Bowl as a player, assistant coach, and head coach. Flores played quarterback for 10 seasons in the AFL with the Raiders, Buffalo Bills, and Kansas City Chiefs. He was a player on the Super Bowl IV-champion Chiefs, an assistant for the Super Bowl XI-champion Raiders, and won Super Bowls XV and XVIII as the Raiders' head coach.

Flores is an accomplished cook, but he says he learned to cook mainly because, "I like to eat." He says it was during his playing days that he realized it was time to get skilled in the kitchen. "There were three of us sharing an apartment," he says. "We would go out to the store, buy three round steaks, and broil them. We'd end up chewing each piece for what seemed like a half an hour. That's when I began experimenting and found out how much fun it is to try creative things, to improvise with your own touches. Now my challenge is to try to duplicate dishes I've had in restaurants."

Dijon Chicken with Gorgonzola

- 1 boneless chicken breast, skinned and split
- 1 egg, beaten
- ½ cup flour
- 2 Tbs butter or margarine
- 6 green onions, finely chopped
- ½ cup chicken broth
- ⅛ tsp fresh oregano, minced
- ⅛ tsp fresh cilantro, minced
- 1 Tbs white wine
- 1 Tbs Dijon mustard
- 4 oz Gorgonzola cheese, crumbled

1. Pound the chicken breast halves to tenderize them. Dip them in egg, then dredge in flour.
2. In a large sauté pan, melt the butter or margarine. Sauté the chicken breasts until golden brown. Remove the chicken and set aside.
3. Add the green onions to the pan and sauté for 30-45 seconds (add more butter, if necessary). Add the chicken broth, oregano, and cilantro. Continue to sauté, and add the wine and Dijon mustard. Stir to blend well. Simmer for two-three minutes.
4. Sprinkle a little of the leftover flour in the mixture to thicken it as it cooks. Do not make the sauce too thick, however.
5. Fold in the gorgonzola and stir until the sauce is smooth.
6. To serve: Put a tablespoon of the sauce on each of two serving plates and spread out slightly. Put a chicken breast half on top of the sauce. Then pour more sauce on top of the chicken. Serve with rice and fresh vegetables.

MARINADE:
- ¼ cup soy sauce
- 3 Tbs honey
- 2 Tbs white vinegar
- 1 ½ tsp garlic powder
- 1 ½ tsp powdered ginger
- ¾ cup vegetable oil
- 3-4 green onions, chopped
- 1 flank steak (about 1 ½ lbs average)

Marinated Flank Steak

1. In a large mason jar or covered bowl, mix together all the marinade ingredients. Shake or stir well to combine.

2. Pour the marinade over the steak, cover, and refrigerate overnight.

3. Prepare a barbecue or outdoor grill. When the coals are hot, remove the steak from the marinade. Place the steak on the barbecue and grill for 5 minutes on each side with the hood down or cover on. Slice and serve.

Tim Bream

HEAD TRAINER, CHICAGO BEARS

Tim Bream joined the Bears in 1993 after 10 years as a college trainer at Syracuse, Vanderbilt, and the University of Richmond. Bream's first NFL experience was as an intern for the Detroit Lions in 1981. He graduated from Penn State and has a master's degree from West Virginia.

Who ever heard of putting corn flakes in chocolate chip cookies? "That's what makes them crunchy," says Lisa Bream, wife of Bears head trainer Tim Bream. "I can't claim credit for the idea, though. The recipe came from a friend years ago." Lisa, who loves to bake, occasionally sends a plate of cookies to the Bears' facility. "The players and coaches love them," she says. "Sometimes there are even a few left for the office staff." Besides Tim, Lisa also has two other cookie monsters in the house, daughters Rebecca, 6, and Elizabeth, 2.

"They help me bake," Lisa says.

Crunchy Chocolate Chip Cookies

1. Preheat oven to 350 degrees. In a large mixing bowl, cream together the butter or margarine and the two sugars. Add the egg, milk, oil, and vanilla, and mix well with a wooden spoon.

2. Add the flour, baking soda, salt, oats, and corn flakes. Mix well. Then add the chocolate chips and the walnuts. Mix again to evenly distribute the chocolate chips and walnuts.

3. Drop the dough by rounded teaspoonfuls, 2 inches apart, onto an ungreased cookie sheet. Bake each batch for 8-10 minutes. Cool on a baking rack or plate.

- 1 cup butter or margarine, softened
- 1 cup white sugar
- 1 cup brown sugar
- 1 egg
- 1 Tbs milk
- 1 cup vegetable oil
- 2 tsp vanilla
- 3½ cups flour
- 3 tsp baking soda
- 1 tsp salt
- 1 cup rolled oats
- 1 cup cornflakes, crushed
- 1 package (12 oz) chocolate chips
- 1 cup walnut pieces

Jack Kemp

QUARTERBACK, SAN DIEGO CHARGERS 1960-62, BUFFALO BILLS 1962-69

Before taking on a leadership role in government, Jack Kemp was a leader in the NFL at quarterback for the San Diego Chargers and Buffalo Bills. In his 10-year pro football career, Kemp played in five AFL Championship Games, three with the Bills and two with the Chargers. He was named AFL player of the year in 1965 after leading the Bills to a second consecutive title. Kemp, a nine-term U.S. Congressman from New York state, served as Secretary of Housing and Urban Development from 1989-1992. In 1996, Kemp was Republican Presidential candidate Bob Dole's Vice Presidential running mate.

CAKE:
- 3 cups flour
- 2 cups sugar
- ½ cup cocoa
- 1 tsp salt
- 2 tsp baking soda
- 2 tsp vinegar
- 2 cups cold water
- 2 tsp vanilla
- ⅔ cup vegetable oil

FROSTING:
- 2 squares unsweetened chocolate
- 6 Tbs butter, softened
- 1-2 Tbs corn syrup
- 1 tsp vanilla
- 1 box powdered sugar
- milk as needed

Moist Chocolate Cake

1. Preheat oven to 350 degrees.

2. In a large bowl, mix the flour, sugar, cocoa, salt, and baking soda until well blended.

3. Add the vinegar, water, vanilla, and oil. Mix until smooth.

4. Pour the cake batter into a 9" x 12" ungreased cake pan. Bake for 30 minutes or until the top bounces back when touched. Cool the cake.

5. To make the frosting, melt the chocolate in a medium saucepan and mix with the butter. Add the corn syrup, vanilla, and powdered sugar. Gradually add milk until the desired consistency for spreading is reached.

6. Spread frosting over the cooled cake.

Pro Football Champions

National Football League Champions 1920-1969

1969	Minnesota Vikings	**1944**	Green Bay Packers
1968	Baltimore Colts	**1943**	Chicago Bears
1967	Green Bay Packers	**1942**	Washington Redskins
1966	Green Bay Packers	**1941**	Chicago Bears
1965	Green Bay Packers	**1940**	Chicago Bears
1964	Cleveland Browns	**1939**	Green Bay Packers
1963	Chicago Bears	**1938**	New York Giants
1962	Green Bay Packers	**1937**	Washington Redskins
1961	Green Bay Packers	**1936**	Green Bay Packers
1960	Philadelphia Eagles	**1935**	Detroit Lions
1959	Baltimore Colts	**1934**	New York Giants
1958	Baltimore Colts	**1933**	Chicago Bears
1957	Detroit Lions	**1932**	Chicago Bears
1956	New York Giants	**1931**	Green Bay Packers
1955	Cleveland Browns	**1930**	Green Bay Packers
1954	Cleveland Browns	**1929**	Green Bay Packers
1953	Detroit Lions	**1928**	Providence Steam Roller
1952	Detroit Lions	**1927**	New York Giants
1951	Los Angeles Rams	**1926**	Frankford Yellow Jackets
1950	Cleveland Browns	**1925**	Chicago Cardinals
1949	Philadelphia Eagles	**1924**	Cleveland Bulldogs
1948	Philadelphia Eagles	**1923**	Canton Bulldogs
1947	Chicago Cardinals	**1922**	Canton Bulldogs
1946	Chicago Bears	**1921**	Chicago Staleys
1945	Cleveland Rams	**1920**	Akron Pros

1956 NFL Championship Game:
New York Giants 47, Chicago Bears 7

American Football League Champions 1960-1969

1969 Kansas City Chiefs		**1964** Buffalo Bills	
1968 New York Jets		**1963** San Diego Chargers	
1967 Oakland Raiders		**1962** Dallas Texans	
1966 Kansas City Chiefs		**1961** Houston Oilers	
1965 Buffalo Bills		**1960** Houston Oilers	

REGULAR SEASON

Steve Largent
- Saturday Morning Waffles

Kerry Collins
- Grandma Collins's Irish Soda Bread

Stan Humphries
- Easy Shrimp Dip

John Friesz
- Quarterback Stew

Franco Harris
- Immaculate Lasagna

Ron Blackledge
- Zucchini Proudone

Wayne Chrebet
- Meatball Stew

Ronnie Lott
- Lotta Spicy Pasta

Joe Wolf
- BBQ Beef Sandwiches

Ty Detmer
- Fried Venison Backstrap

George Martin
- Chicken Dianne

Bud Grant
- Pheasant and Wild Rice Casserole
- Kangaroo Cookies

Glenn Parker
- Chicken Chile Rellenos

Tom Matte
- Italian Sausage Soup With Tortellini
- Scallops Parisian
- Tom Matte's Chili

Keith Sims
- Pumpkin Bars

Howie Long
- Apple Pie

Immaculate Lasagna

Steve Largent

WIDE RECEIVER, SEATTLE SEAHAWKS 1976-1989

Largent may not have been the quickest or fastest receiver in the game, but he was one of the all-time best. When he retired in 1989, Largent had accumulated then-NFL-record totals of 100 touchdown receptions, 819 career receptions, and 13,089 receiving yards. Largent (R-Oklahoma) currently is a member of the U.S. House of Representatives.

This is a recipe that Congressman Largent says he often makes when it is his turn to cook at home.

Saturday Morning Waffles

1. Preheat the waffle iron.
2. In a large bowl, mix all the ingredients together until there are no lumps. Add more flour as necessary to achieve a thick pouring consistency.
3. Pour the batter into the waffle iron and cook until golden brown.
4. Serve the waffles with maple syrup and your favorite fresh fruit.

- 2 cups sifted flour
- ⅓ cup sugar
- 1 tsp salt
- 4 tsp baking powder
- 3 eggs
- 2½ cups milk
- ½ cup vegetable oil
- 1-2 tsp vanilla

 EXTRA POINT: This waffle batter will keep in the refrigerator for up to five days.

Kerry Collins

QUARTERBACK, CAROLINA PANTHERS

As a senior at Penn State in 1994, Collins led the Nittany Lions to the Rose Bowl. In 1996, he directed the Carolina Panthers to within one game of the Super Bowl in their second season in the NFL. He has emerged as one of the league's bright young quarterbacks. Collins, the first selection of the Panthers (fifth overall) in the 1995 NFL draft, has a 16-9 record as a starter in his first two NFL seasons.

This soda bread is one of Collins's fondest childhood memories. "I would go to my grandmother's house on Sundays and I'd watch her make this bread," he says. "I still remember how wonderful the house would smell while it was baking."

Grandma Collins's Irish Soda Bread

- 4 cups all-purpose flour
- 3 Tbs sugar
- 1 Tbs baking powder
- 1 tsp salt
- 1 tsp baking soda
- 6 Tbs butter or margarine (¾ stick)
- 1 ½ cups golden raisins
- 2 eggs
- 1 ½ cups buttermilk

1. Preheat oven to 350 degrees. Grease a round 2-quart casserole dish.

2. In a large mixing bowl, mix the dry ingredients (flour, sugar, baking powder, salt, and baking soda).

3. With a pastry blender, heavy-duty mixer, or 2 knives used scissor-fashion, cut in the butter or margarine until the mixture resembles coarse crumbs. Stir in the raisins.

4. In a measuring cup, lightly beat the eggs. Remove 1 tablespoon of the beaten eggs and reserve.

5. Stir the beaten eggs and the buttermilk into the flour mixture just until the flour is moistened. (The dough will be sticky.)

6. Turn the dough onto a well-floured surface. With well-floured hands, knead the dough 8-10 times to mix thoroughly. Shape the dough into a ball and place in the greased casserole dish. In the top center of the ball, cut a 4-inch cross, about one-fourth inch deep. Brush the dough with the reserved tablespoon of beaten egg.

7. Bake the bread for 1 hour and 20 minutes, or until a toothpick inserted in the center of the loaf comes out clean. Cool in the casserole on a wire rack for 10 minutes. Remove the bread from the casserole and finish cooling on the rack.

 EXTRA POINT: Other dried fruit—dried cranberries or currants—will work in this bread recipe in place of the raisins.

Stan Humphries

QUARTERBACK, SAN DIEGO CHARGERS

Humphries has been the Chargers' starting quarterback since he was acquired in a trade with Washington in 1992. San Diego has reached the playoffs in three of his five seasons with the team, highlighted by an AFC championship in 1994 and an appearance in Super Bowl XXIX. San Diego is 44-24 in games Humphries has started, the second-highest winning percentage among active NFL quarterbacks during that period.

"Stan doesn't care much for shrimp," says Stan's wife, Connie. "So I get to eat this all by myself. Ha!"

- **1 package (3 oz) cream cheese**
- **1 cup sour cream**
- **2 tsp lemon juice**
- **1 package dry Italian salad dressing mix**
- **½-1 cup cooked shrimp, chopped (or bay shrimp)**

Easy Shrimp Dip

1. Rinse shrimp with cool water and dry well.

2. In a small mixing bowl, blend the cream cheese and sour cream.

3. Add the other ingredients and mix well.

4. Chill for 1 hour or more before serving. Serve with your choice of chips or crackers.

John Friesz

QUARTERBACK, SEATTLE SEAHAWKS

In 1995, John Friesz joined the Seattle Seahawks, where he was reunited with Dennis Erickson, his former college coach for one season at Idaho. Friesz set 24 school records at Idaho, along with 18 conference, and five NCAA Division I-AA records. Originally drafted by the Chargers in 1990, Friesz spent four years in San Diego before playing the 1994 season with the Redskins.

"I'm not a gourmet cook," admits Friesz. "Fajitas are my specialty and that's about as fancy as I get." But Friesz's mother, Mary Jo, can cook up a storm, and "Quarterback Stew" is one of her best dishes. "Originally the recipe had no name," Friesz says. "My mom passed it along to a friend of hers at the bank where she worked. The woman had a son who was a fan of mine. She told the boy that the recipe was from John the quarterback's mom. And from then on it was 'Quarterback Stew.'"

*John Friesz
with his mother, Mary Jo,
and his son, Hunter*

Quarterback Stew

1. Soak the beans overnight. Rinse and drain.
2. Place all the stew ingredients in a crock pot on high for two hours, then turn to low. In lieu of a crock pot, cook covered in a large stew pot the same way—over high heat for two hours, then on a low simmer.
3. When the pork is tender, shred the meat and put it back in the pot. Continue cooking for a total of 8-10 hours over low heat, stirring occasionally. Uncover for the last hour prior to serving.
4. In individual serving bowls, ladle the stew over a bed of bite-size corn chips. Serve accompanied with bowls of toppings, including shredded lettuce, chopped onion, diced tomatoes, shredded cheese, sour cream, and salsa.

FOR THE STEW:
- 1 ½ lbs boneless pork roast
- 1 lb dry pinto beans
- 6 cups water
- ½ cup onion, chopped
- 2 cloves garlic chopped
- 1 Tbs salt
- 2 Tbs chili powder
- 1 Tbs cumin
- 1 tsp oregano
- 1 4-oz can green chiles, diced
- Corn chips

TOPPINGS:
- Lettuce, shredded
- Onion, chopped
- Tomatoes, diced
- Monterey Jack or Longhorn cheddar cheese, shredded
- Sour cream
- Salsa

 EXTRA POINT: Because the corn chips are salty, be careful not to add too much salt to the stew while it cooks.

Franco Harris

**RUNNING BACK, PITTSBURGH STEELERS (1972-1983),
SEATTLE SEAHAWKS (1984)**

Harris was a dominant force in the Pittsburgh Steelers' dynasty that won four Super Bowls in the 1970s. In 13 seasons, he rushed for 12,120 yards and 100 touchdowns. Harris was named MVP of Super Bowl IX. His legendary "Immaculate Reception" in the 1972 AFC Divisional Playoff Game against Oakland gave the Steelers their first-ever postseason victory.

Life has become one big road game for Harris. "I keep meaning to cook more," he says, "but I just don't have the time. I'm always on the road." When he does have the time, Franco often makes his famous lasagna. "People seem to really enjoy it," Harris says. "It's always in demand when I entertain and at holiday gatherings." Harris says that his mother, who is Italian, is an excellent cook. "Some of her relatives who still live in Italy are amazing cooks," he adds. "I go every year to visit, and no matter how hard we try here in America, we just can't seem to get the same flavors."

- 2 Tbs olive oil
- 3 large cloves garlic, finely chopped
- 1 lb ground round steak
- 1 large can (29 oz) tomato puree
- 1 large onion, cut into large pieces
- 1 6-oz can tomato paste, plus 1 can water
- ½ tsp dried oregano
- ½ tsp dried basil
- ¼ cup dry red wine
- 2 tsp salt
- ½ cup fresh Romano cheese, grated
- 1 box (1 lb) lasagna noodles
- 1 lb ricotta cheese
- 9 oz mozzarella cheese, shredded

Immaculate Lasagna

1. Preheat oven to 350 degrees. Lightly grease a 9" x 13" baking pan.

2. Heat the olive oil in a large skillet along with the meat. As you cook the meat, crumble it into tiny pieces. Drain off the grease.

3. In a food processor, combine the tomato puree and onion, and process until smooth. Add this to the skillet with the meat and with all the other ingredients except the noodles and cheeses. Cover and simmer for 10 minutes.

4. Cover the bottom of the baking pan with one-third of the meat mixture. Add one-third of the grated Romano cheese. Lay 5 *uncooked* lasagna noodles lengthwise and one crosswise at the top to fill the pan.

5. Spread half of the ricotta cheese over the noodles. Then add half of the shredded mozzarella cheese over the ricotta. Repeat all the layers, ending with the meat sauce and Romano cheese on top.

6. Cover the pan tightly with foil and bake for 1 hour. Remove the foil and let the lasagna stand for 10-20 minutes before serving.

Ron Blackledge

OFFENSIVE LINE COACH, INDIANAPOLIS COLTS

Ron Blackledge spent 10 seasons as the offensive line coach of the Pittsburgh Steelers before joining the Colts in 1992. He played both tight end and defensive end at Bowling Green (1957-59), and later was inducted into the school's Hall of Fame. Prior to joining Chuck Noll's staff in Pittsburgh, Blackledge was the head coach at Kent State from 1979-1981. His son, Todd, was an NFL quarterback with the Kansas City Chiefs and now is a studio analyst for ABC's college football telecasts.

Zucchini Proudone

1. Preheat oven to 350 degrees. Trim the ends off the zucchini, then cut the zucchini into one-eighth-inch slices.

2. In a large frying pan, saute the zucchini, onion, and mushrooms in the olive oil until the vegetables are tender.

3. Remove the pan from the heat and mix in half the Parmesan cheese.

4. In a small mixing bowl, combine the tomato sauce and the seasonings. Add the tomato sauce to the pan with the zucchini mixture, then pour into a 2-quart casserole dish. Sprinkle with the remaining one-third cup of Parmesan cheese.

5. Bake, uncovered, 30-45 minutes, or until the casserole is bubbly.

- 3-4 medium zucchini (approximately 2 lbs)
- ½ cup onion, chopped
- 1 can (4 oz) mushrooms (or 4 oz fresh, sliced)
- 3 Tbs olive oil
- ⅔ cup Parmesan cheese, grated
- 1 can (15 oz) tomato sauce
- dash of garlic powder
- ½-1 tsp salt (to taste)
- ⅛ tsp black pepper
- ½ tsp monosodium glutamate (optional)

Wayne Chrebet

WIDE RECEIVER, NEW YORK JETS

Chrebet is the only player in NFL history to catch 150 passes in his first two seasons. He led the Jets with 84 receptions in 1996, despite starting only nine games. Chrebet joined the Jets in 1995 as a free agent out of Hofstra, then caught 66 passes to break the club record for receptions by a rookie. In his senior season at Hofstra, he tied Jerry Rice's NCAA record with 5 touchdowns against Delaware.

It is a wonder Chrebet likes cooking at all after what happened to him one summer. "When I was nine," he says, "my dad and I were at our summer house. My dad had bought a brand new gas barbecue grill. While my dad wasn't looking, I turned on the grill and closed the cover. My dad struck a match to light the grill and the whole thing exploded. The grill and cover flew about forty feet in the air and the flames singed our eyebrows and the hair on our arms. When the grill came down, it no longer had any paint on it and the cover was completely burned. That was my first cooking experience."

- **3 lbs ground chuck**
- **3 eggs**
- **3 slices of white bread, broken into small pieces**
- **2 Tbs vegetable oil**
- **5 lbs potatoes**
- **1 large onion, finely chopped**
- **salt and pepper to taste**
- **1 can or jar beef gravy or 1 packet dry beef gravy mix**

Meatball Stew

1. In a large mixing bowl, combine the ground chuck, eggs, and bread. Form the mixture into meatballs (approximately 1-inch in diameter). In a large frying pan, brown the meatballs in the oil.

2. Remove the meatballs from the frying pan with a slotted spoon and place in the bottom of a large stew pot. Cover the meatballs with water. Add the potatoes and onions to the pot, and season with salt and pepper to taste. Cover the pot and bring to a boil. Then lower the heat and simmer until the potatoes are tender.

3. Add the gravy or the prepared gravy mix. Simmer for another few minutes before serving.

Ronnie Lott

DEFENSIVE BACK, SAN FRANCISCO 49ERS 1981-1990, LOS ANGELES RAIDERS 1991-92, NEW YORK JETS 1993-94

Ferocious hits and a keen sense for the ball were Lott's trademarks during his 14-year career in the NFL. Lott was the defensive leader for the 49ers' four Super Bowl championship teams in the 1980s. He led the NFL in interceptions in 1986 with San Francisco, and again in 1991 as a member of the Raiders. Lott is the 49ers' career leader in interceptions. He rejoined his former Raiders teammate Howie Long as Fox *NFL Sunday* studio analysts in 1996.

"Ronnie loves pasta and Ronnie loves spice," says Karen Lott. "Spice is the key in our family. We tend to put red pepper flakes in everything." Well, maybe not everything. "I have three little kids," she says, "so when I make this pasta dish, I take out some of the penne when it's cooked and just butter the noodles for them." Karen says that she and her mother "read cookbooks like novels." "My recipes vary daily," she says. "It just depends on what's in the garden or the cupboard."

Ronnie gives daughter Chloe a cooking lesson.

- **6 mild Italian sausages**
- **2 Tbs unsalted butter**
- **1 medium onion, chopped**
- **1 ½ tsp red pepper flakes**
- **2 cans whole Italian plum tomatoes (1 lb each), juice included**
- **1 cup vodka**
- **1 cup whipping cream**
- **1 Tbs tomato paste**
- **1 pound penne pasta**
- **1 cup Parmesan cheese**
- **fresh oregano, chopped, to taste**

Lotta Spicy Pasta

1. Bring water to a boil in a large pot. Add the sausages and cook for 10 minutes. Remove from the pot and cool. Discard the water.

2. Melt the butter in a large sauté pan over medium heat. Add the onions and red pepper flakes and cook until onions are soft. Add the tomatoes, reduce heat and simmer for 1 hour.

3. Cut the sausages into bite-size pieces, then add with the vodka to the saute pan and simmer for 10-15 minutes. Turn heat to high and add the cream and tomato paste. Stir and cook for 10-15 minutes.

4. Boil the pasta in a large pot, following the cooking directions on the package.

5. Drain the pasta and put in a large serving bowl. Add the tomato-sausage mixture and sprinkle with Parmesan cheese and fresh oregano.

Joe Wolf

GUARD/TACKLE, ARIZONA CARDINALS

Wolf has been one of the Cardinals' most versatile offensive linemen. Arizona's first-round pick in the 1989 NFL draft, Wolf played three different positions during his rookie season. In 1996, Wolf started every game at right tackle. At Boston College, he was on the line that protected 1984 Heisman Trophy-winning quarterback Doug Flutie.

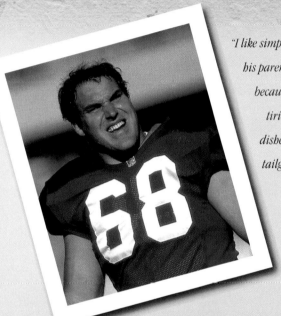

"I like simple food," Wolf says. "I'm not really into anything with fancy sauces." As a teenager his parents let him do some of the cooking on the family barbecue. He later learned to cook because he lived alone. "It was either cook or go out every night," he says, "and that gets tiring." Wolf still does most of the cooking on the grill, but he leaves more complicated dishes to his wife Jean Marie. "This barbecued beef recipe is a natural for game-day or tailgate parties," Joe says. "You just keep it warm and serve it on kaiser rolls or buns."

- 2 lbs ground beef
- 2 large onions, chopped
- 1 tsp vegetable oil
- 2 Tbs flour
- 2 Tbs sugar (or less to taste)
- 1 tsp salt
- ¼ tsp pepper
- 2 cups ketchup
- 2 tsp Worcestershire sauce

BBQ Beef Sandwiches

1. In a large frying pan, brown the meat and onions in the oil over moderate heat. Remove from the heat and pour off the fat.
2. Combine flour, sugar, salt, and pepper. Sprinkle over the meat and stir. Add the ketchup and Worcestershire sauce and stir.
3. Return the pan to the stove. Cover and simmer over low heat for 20 minutes.
4. Serve as a filling for sandwiches on your favorite rolls or in hamburger or hot dog buns.

 EXTRA POINT: If you like your dishes spicier, substitute barbecue sauce for ½-1 cup of the ketchup. Or add a few drops of pepper sauce while the barbecued beef is simmering.

Ty Detmer

QUARTERBACK, PHILADELPHIA EAGLES

Ty Detmer had his finest season as a pro in 1996. The former Heisman Trophy winner from Brigham Young filled in for Rodney Peete, who was injured, and passed for 2,911 yards and 15 touchdowns, leading Philadelphia to its second consecutive playoff appearance. Prior to joining the Eagles in 1996 as a free agent, Detmer spent four seasons in Green Bay.

Detmer grew up hunting and fishing with his dad in San Antonio, Texas. "When I was ten or twelve, I got to go along on hunts," Detmer says. "When we got home, my mom would cook up our game. Venison was a big part of our diet." Detmer says he likes the backstrap because it is such a tender cut of meat. "This recipe is a lot like chicken-fried steak," he says. "My mom used to roll the meat in plain flour. I like my meat spicy, so I add seasoning to the flour. If there are any leftovers, I whip up a little cream gravy and pour it on." Detmer doesn't get much time for hunting because another season—football—takes precedence over deer season in the fall. But he does manage to get out on occasional Tuesdays, his day off. "I generally cook the meat around our house," he says. "My wife Kim cooks everything else. I guess being from Texas I just like to grill and barbecue."

- 1 venison tenderloin (beef tenderloin may be substituted)
- 1 egg
- 1 cup milk
- 1 cup flour
- 1 tsp seasoned salt, or to taste
- ⅛ tsp cayenne pepper or chili powder, or to taste (optional)
- 2 Tbs olive oil

Fried Venison Backstrap

1. Cut the venison backstrap into half-inch slices.

2. Mix the egg and milk in a small bowl. Beat lightly.

3. Mix the flour with the seasoned salt and cayenne or chili powder. Dip the venison slices in the egg mixture, then in flour, shaking off any excess.

4. Heat the olive oil in a large, heavy skillet. Fry the venison slices for 5 minutes per side.

EXTRA POINT: Venison now is farm raised (often imported from New Zealand) and available in many areas. If you can't find venison in your local market, filet mignon or a similar tender cut of beef can be substituted for backstrap.

*Kim and Ty Detmer
with daughters Aubri and Kailis*

George Martin

DEFENSIVE END, NEW YORK GIANTS 1975-1988

Martin was an eleventh-round draft choice in 1975 who became a mainstay of the New York Giants' defense. He was a standout defensive end for the Giants' team that won Super Bowl XXI; Martin tackled Denver quarterback John Elway in the end zone for a safety in that game. Remarkably, Martin scored 7 touchdowns in his 14-year career in the NFL.

This recipe is named for Martin's wife Dianne, who developed it. "If it were named for who consumed most of it," he says, "it would be named after me. We're originally from the South, where chicken is a mainstay. But we wanted to get away from fried foods, and Dianne came up with this, which is a wonderful substitute." There's another reason George likes Chicken Dianne so much. "We have two grown kids and two teenagers living at home," he says. "This dish is a good, hearty meal."

Chicken Dianne

- **2 eggs, beaten**
- **4 whole boneless chicken breasts, skinned and split**
- **1 cup Italian bread crumbs**
- **4 Tbs butter, melted**
- **8 oz fresh mushrooms, sliced**
- **¾ cup Muenster cheese, grated**
- **1 can (10 ¾ oz) chicken broth**
- **1 can (10 ¾ oz) cream of mushroom soup**

1. Preheat oven to 350 degrees.

2. Pour the beaten eggs into a medium mixing bowl. Dip the chicken breasts in the egg, then coat with the bread crumbs.

3. In a large frying pan, melt the butter. Saute the chicken until golden brown. Transfer the chicken to a 9" x 13" baking dish.

4. Cover the chicken with the mushrooms, then sprinkle on the cheese.

5. In a separate mixing bowl or large measuring cup, mix the broth and the cream of mushroom soup. Whisk to remove any lumps. Pour the soup mixture over the chicken.

6. Bake for 30-35 minutes.

 EXTRA POINT: You can use different types of cheeses to vary the flavor of this recipe. Monterey Jack works well, as does sharp Cheddar, or a combination of the two.

George and Dianne Martin

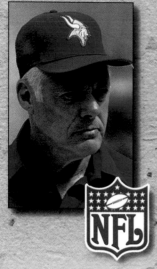

Bud Grant

HEAD COACH, MINNESOTA VIKINGS (1967-1983, 1985)

In the six years prior to Grant's arrival in Minnesota, the Vikings had just one winning season. During his 18 seasons as head coach, Minnesota won 11 division titles, the 1969 NFL Championship, and NFC championships in 1973, 1974, and 1976. Grant's teams played in four Super Bowls. Grant, a superb athlete, played professional basketball for the NBA's Minneapolis Lakers before signing with the NFL's Philadelphia Eagles as an end. He was elected to the Pro Football Hall of Fame in 1994.

Grant is an avid outdoorsman, hunter, and fisherman. Consequently, his wife, Pat, has developed an extensive wild game and fish recipe file. The Pheasant and Wild Rice Casserole is one of her preferred fall dishes.

Kangaroo Cookies

1. Preheat oven to 350 degrees.
2. Blend the butter, one-half cup of the brown sugar, and the vanilla. Beat in the egg yolks.
3. Add the flour, alternating with the water. Mix in the chocolate chips.
4. Beat the egg whites until stiff and add the remaining one-half cup brown sugar. Fold into the chocolate chip dough.
5. Spread the dough into greased a 13" x 9" baking pan and bake for 30 minutes.
6. Sprinkle with powdered sugar while still warm. Cool and cut into serving squares.

- 1 cup butter
- 1 cup brown sugar
- 2 tsp vanilla
- 2 eggs, separated
- 2 cups flour
- ½ cup water
- 1 package (12 oz) chocolate chips
- ¼ cup powdered sugar

Pheasant and Wild Rice Casserole

- 6 oz wild rice
- 3 cups pheasant, cooked and cubed
- 1 can (10¾ oz) cream of chicken soup
- 1 can (6½ oz) sliced water chestnuts
- 1 can (8 oz) sliced mushrooms
- 3 Tbs soy sauce
- ½ cup water

Pheasant and Wild Rice Casserole

1. Preheat oven to 350 degrees.

2. Cook the rice according to package directions. Combine with all the other ingredients and place in a covered casserole dish.

3. Bake covered for 1 hour.

 EXTRA POINT: Turkey may be used as a substitute for the pheasant, making this an excellent recipe for Thanksgiving leftovers.

Glenn Parker

GUARD-TACKLE, BUFFALO BILLS

Parker has done all right for a guy who didn't start playing football competitively until he attended Golden West (Junior) College in Huntington Beach, California. He went on to play at the University of Arizona, where he was named All-Pacific10 in 1989, and was Buffalo's third-round draft choice in 1990. Parker has developed into a major component of the Bills' offensive line and has started in three of Buffalo's four Super Bowl appearances.

When you cook with green chiles, even the relatively mild forms such as poblanos, *it is difficult to know exactly how hot they are. "After you roast the chiles for my Chile Rellenos," Parker suggests, "take a tiny taste of each one to test their heat. The last time I made chile rellenos for a dinner party, two of them were really hot. Luckily, my wife and I got them." Parker, who says he does most of the cooking at home, learned Southwestern cooking while he was attending Arizona and on trips with his parents, who own a vacation home in Mexico.*

- 8-10 whole fresh *poblano* chiles
- 2 chicken breast halves, boned and skinned
- 8 oz Monterey Jack cheese (or queso fresco, *where available*)
- ½ cup whole kernel corn, sliced off the cob
- fresh ground black pepper to taste
- ⅔ cup flour
- 2 eggs, beaten
- ⅓ cup milk
- ⅓ cup beer
- ½ tsp salt
- vegetable oil for frying
- sour cream for garnish
  ADOBO SEASONING:
- ½ tsp salt
- 1 large clove garlic, minced
- ¼ tsp oregano
- ⅛ tsp black pepper
- ⅛ tsp turmeric
  PICO DE GALLO SALSA:
- 1-2 *serrano* chiles
- 3 ripe tomatoes, diced
- 1 small onion, diced
- 2 Tbs cilantro, finely chopped
- 1 Tbs fresh lime juice

Chicken Chile Rellenos

1. Roast the *poblano* chiles by blackening the skin on all sides under the broiler or over an open flame. Put the hot chiles into a brown paper bag or sealed plastic container until cooled. Peel the blackened skin from the chiles, being careful not to tear the flesh underneath or to remove the stems. Cut a small slit lengthwise in each of the chiles and through it remove the seeds. Set the chiles aside.

2. In a large pot, boil the chicken until cooked through (about 20 minutes). Drain and cool. Shred the chicken meat.

3. Place 2 cups of the shredded chicken in a medium bowl. Add the cheese, corn, *adobo* seasoning, and black pepper to taste. Combine well until mixture has a pasty consistency.

4. Through the slits you made in the chiles, fill each chile with a tablespoon or two of the chicken-cheese mixture. Set aside.

5. Begin to make a *pico de gallo* salsa by seeding and finely dicing the *serrano* chile. In a bowl, mix the diced *serrano* chile, tomatoes, onion, and cilantro. Add the lime juice, and salt and pepper to taste. The mixture should have a relish-like texture. Set aside.

6. In a large bowl, mix the flour, eggs, milk, beer, and salt, plus pepper to taste. Combine well until the mixture is the consistency of pancake batter.

7. Heat the oil in a large skillet. When the oil is hot, dip each
   stuffed chile into the batter. Fry the chiles in the oil until golden brown.
8. To serve, put a small amount of *pico de gallo* salsa on each plate. Place a chile
   on top of the salsa and garnish with the optional sour cream and a sprig of
   fresh cilantro.

Tom Matte

HALFBACK, BALTIMORE COLTS (1961-1972)

Matte, a running back and former Ohio State quarterback, gained 116 yards on 11 carries in Super Bowl III. He was an emergency quarterback in place of injured Johnny Unitas and Gary Cuozzo in Baltimore's final game of the 1965 season, when he led the Colts to a victory over the Rams to tie Green Bay for the Western Conference title. A week later, with the plays taped to his wrist, Matte nearly pulled off another miracle. But Baltimore lost 13-10 in overtime to eventual NFL Champion Green Bay.

Matte says he always has had an interest in cooking: "My father was a good cook, and I still swap recipes with my brother, who played pro football and baseball." Matte, who at one time was in the restaurant business, comes from what he calls "a soup family." "In the fall, we begin making a lot of soups," he says, "including this Italian Sausage Soup with Tortellini. A soup like that is a meal in itself."

- 1 lb Italian sausage (½ lb sweet and ½ lb hot recommended)
- 1 Tbs olive oil
- 1 cup onion, coarsely chopped
- 4-6 garlic cloves, thinly sliced
- 2 cups beef broth
- ½ cup water
- ½ cup dry red wine
- 1 can (8 oz) tomato sauce
- 4 medium tomatoes, peeled, seeded, and chopped
- 1 cup small zucchini, thinly sliced
- 1 cup carrots, thinly sliced
- ½ tsp basil
- ¾ tsp oregano
- 8 oz fresh meat- or cheese-filled tortellini (or 2 cups frozen)
- 3 Tbs Italian parsley, minced
- grated Parmesan cheese, to taste

Italian Sausage Soup With Tortellini

1. Remove the sausage from the casings. In a heavy skillet, sauté until cooked through. Drain off any grease.

2. In a large, heavy-bottomed soup pot, sauté the onions and garlic in the olive oil until the onions are soft. Add the sausage, broth, water, wine, and tomato sauce. Bring to a boil, then reduce to simmer.

3. Add the tomatoes, carrots, zucchini, basil, and oregano. Simmer until the vegetables are tender, 45 minutes to 1 hour.

4. Add the tortellini to the pot approximately 10 minutes before serving (depending on the type of tortellini used; follow package cooking directions if not using fresh tortellini).

5. Serve the soup in bowls. Sprinkle a little parsley on the top of each serving along with grated Parmesan cheese, if desired.

Tom Matte checks his wristband for the correct ingredients.

Scallops Parisian

- 1 ½ cups dry white wine
- bouquet garni
- 2 lbs large sea scallops, washed and drained
- salt, to taste
- 2 Tbs plus 4 Tbs butter
- 2 Tbs water
- ½ lb fresh mushrooms, cleaned and chopped
- 6 shallots, minced
- 1 Tbs parsley, minced
- 1 tsp lemon juice
- ¼ cup flour
- 2 egg yolks
- ¼ cup heavy cream
- ½ cup bread crumbs

1. Preheat oven to 400 degrees. Put the wine and bouquet garni in a large saucepan. Bring to a boil. Add the scallops and a little salt to taste, and simmer for 3 minutes, or until the scallops are tender. Remove the scallops and reserve the broth. Cut the scallops into bite-size pieces and set aside.

2. In a medium saucepan, melt 2 tablespoons of the butter. Add the water, mushrooms, shallots, parsley, and lemon juice. Cover the pan and simmer the mixture for 10 minutes. Strain the liquid and add it to the reserved wine broth. Reserve the mushrooms and shallots.

3. Melt 4 tablespoons butter in a large saucepan. Add the flour and stir completely to make a roux. Gradually add all but 1 tablespoon of the combined broth mixture and stir constantly until it is thick and smooth. Remove the saucepan from the heat.

4. Beat the egg yolks with the cream and the remaining 1 tablespoon of broth. Gently blend the egg yolk mixture into the roux. Stir in the scallops and mushroom-shallot mixture. Taste, then correct the seasoning.

5. Spoon the scallop mixture into 4 to 6 scallop shells or ramekins. Sprinkle with bread crumbs and dot each with some of the remaining butter. Brown lightly in the oven or under the broiler.

 EXTRA POINT: Matte suggests serving this dish with fresh asparagus with Hollandaise sauce and "those funny little potatoes" sautéed in clarified butter and topped with freshly grated Parmesan cheese.

Tom Matte's Chili

- ½ lb dry pinto beans
- 1 lb green bell peppers, seeded and coarsely chopped
- 1 ½ Tbs vegetable oil
- 1 ½ lbs onions, coarsely chopped
- 2 cloves garlic, crushed
- ½ cup parsley, minced
- ½ cup butter
- 2 ½ lbs lean ground beef
- 1 lb lean ground pork
- ⅓ cup chili powder (mild or hot, to taste)
- 5 cups canned tomatoes, drained and chopped (or recipe ready)
- 2 Tbs salt
- 1 ½ tsp pepper
- 1 ½ tsp ground cumin

1. Rinse the beans. Place them in a bowl and cover with about 2 inches of water. Soak the beans overnight.
2. Pour the beans and soaking water into a large heavy-bottomed pot or kettle. Cover and simmer until the beans are tender, 1-2 hours.
3. While the beans are cooking, sauté the green peppers in the oil in a large skillet. Add the onions and cook, stirring until tender. Add the garlic and parsley. Remove from heat.
4. In another large skillet, melt the butter. Add the beef and pork and sauté for about 15 minutes. With a slotted spoon, transfer the meat to the green pepper-onion pan. Stir in the chili powder and simmer for 10 minutes.
5. When the beans are cooked, add the tomatoes to the pot and simmer 5 minutes longer. Add the meat mixture to the beans, and season with salt, pepper, and cumin.
6. Simmer the chili, covered, for 1 hour. Remove the cover and continue cooking for 30 minutes, stirring occasionally and adding water, if necessary, to keep the mixture moistened. Skim any fat before serving.

 EXTRA POINT: This recipe makes approximately four quarts. Chili freezes well: cool, spoon into freezer containers, cover tightly, and freeze.

Keith Sims

GUARD, MIAMI DOLPHINS

Keith Sims has one of the most important jobs in Miami—protecting the blindside of future Pro Football Hall of Fame quarterback Dan Marino. Sims, a four-year starter at Iowa State, was drafted by the Dolphins in the second round of the 1990 NFL draft and became an instant starter. He was selected to three consecutive Pro Bowls from 1993-95.

Sims admits it freely: "My wife considers me a terrible cook and I defer to her." But that doesn't mean he's not a good eater. This Pumpkin Bars recipe is one of his favorites and already has passed the test with his two-year-old daughter, Cairo. "It's kind of like pumpkin pie you can make in any season," he says. Keith and his wife Cammy brought this dish as a potluck dessert for the opening session of a Bible-study class. "It was such a big hit," he says, "we had to bring the dessert for all sixteen weeks the group met."

Pumpkin Bars

1. Preheat oven to 350 degrees.
2. Put all the dry ingredients in a large bowl and combine well.
3. In a separate bowl, beat the eggs. Beat in the sugar, oil, and pumpkin. Blend into the dry ingredients and mix well.
4. Pour into a greased 9" x 12" baking pan. Bake for 30 minutes or until the cake is set.
5. To make the frosting: Combine all frosting ingredients in a large bowl and beat until smooth. Wait until the cake is cooled thoroughly before frosting. Cut into bars.

- 2 cups pre-sifted all-purpose flour
- 2 tsp baking powder
- 1 Tbs baking soda
- ½ tsp salt
- ½ tsp cinnamon
- ½ tsp pumpkin pie spice
- 4 eggs
- 2 cups sugar (or less, to taste)
- 1 cup vegetable oil
- 1 can (15 oz) pumpkin
FROSTING:
- 3 oz cream cheese
- ½ stick butter or margarine
- 2 Tbs milk
- 1 tsp vanilla
- 2 cups powdered sugar
- 2 Tbs solid shortening

EXTRA POINT: Keith says he is "not a big icing fan." He prefers this dish unfrosted, accompanied by vanilla ice cream.

Howie Long

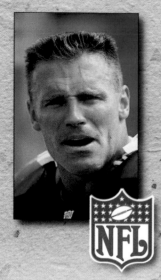

**DEFENSIVE END/TACKLE,
OAKLAND/LOS ANGELES RAIDERS 1981-1993**

Before becoming an Emmy Award-winning analyst on the Fox *NFL Sunday* studio show, Long was one of the NFL's dominant defensive players. During his 13-year NFL career, Long recorded 84 sacks and played in eight Pro Bowls. He was a starting defensive end on the Raiders' Super Bowl XVIII champions. Also an actor, Long co-starred in the 1996 action hit *Broken Arrow*, and will be seen in *Firestorm*, which will be released in 1998.

This apple pie is Diane Long's trademark dessert. "I got the recipe from a friend of mine whose family farmed apples in Washington state," Diane says. "It was her grandmother's recipe. When I first tried it, Howie and I had just gotten married. Now, when I make it, I usually make two pies at a time because it's Howie's favorite. He actually hides the leftovers and threatens anyone who comes near them." Diane says the vinegar crust can be used for both sweet and savory pies. "I make a pecan pie with it," she says, "but I also use it for a number of quiche variations."

Apple Pie

PIE CRUSTS:
- **2 cups flour**
- **½ Tbs sugar**
- **1 Tbs salt**
- **⅚ cup shortening**
- **¼ cup water**
- **1 Tbs cider vinegar**
- **1 egg**

FILLING:
- **¾ cup brown sugar**
- **¾ cup granulated sugar**
- **1 Tbs corn starch**
- **6 cups pippin or Granny Smith apples, peeled and sliced**
- **1 tsp cinnamon**
- **1 Tbs lemon juice**
- **1 Tbs butter**

1. For the crusts, combine the flour, sugar, and salt in a large bowl. Cut in the shortening until coarse.

2. In a separate bowl, combine the water, vinegar, and egg and beat with a fork. Pour into the flour mixture and mix until the pastry holds together.

3. Divide the dough into 2 balls. Cover and chill for at least 2 hours. Roll out each crust until they are 2 inches larger than the pie plate.

4. Preheat oven to 375 degrees. Line a pie plate with one of the crusts.

5. To make the pie filling, mix the sugar and cornstarch in a large bowl.

6. Add the apples, cinnamon, and lemon juice, and toss well. Pour the apple mixture into the pastry-lined pie plate.

7. Dot with butter and cover with the top crust. Seal and flute the edges of the crust, and cut slits in the top of the pie.

8. Bake for 45-50 minutes, until the crust is golden brown.

EXTRA POINT: You can make this dough ahead of time and have it on hand when you want it. Wrap it tightly and refrigerate for up to two weeks, or freeze for up to two months. To thaw the dough, leave wrapped in the refrigerator for 2 hours.

Howie Long changed uniforms and careers.

Super Bowl Chronology

January 26, 1997
Green Bay 35, New England 21
Louisiana Superdome, New Orleans
MVP: Packers KR Desmond Howard

January 26, 1992
Washington 37, Buffalo 24
Metrodome, Minneapolis
MVP: Redskins QB Mark Rypien

January 25, 1987
N.Y. Giants 39, Denver 20
Rose Bowl, Pasadena
MVP: Giants QB Phil Simms

January 28, 1996
Dallas 27, Pittsburgh 17
Sun Devil Stadium, Tempe
MVP: Cowboys CB Larry Brown

January 27, 1991
N.Y. Giants 20, Buffalo 19
Tampa Stadium, Tampa
MVP: Giants RB Ottis Anderson

January 26, 1986
Chicago 46, New England 10
Louisiana Superdome, New Orleans
MVP: Bears DE Richard Dent

January 29, 1995
San Francisco 49, San Diego 26
Joe Robbie Stadium, Miami
MVP: 49ers QB Steve Young

January 28, 1990
San Francisco 55, Denver 10
Louisiana Superdome, New Orleans
MVP: 49ers QB Joe Montana

January 20, 1985
San Francisco 38, Miami 16
Stanford Stadium, Stanford
MVP: 49ers QB Joe Montana

January 30, 1994
Dallas 30, Buffalo 13
Georgia Dome, Atlanta
MVP: Cowboys RB Emmitt Smith

January 22, 1989
San Francisco 20, Cincinnati 16
Joe Robbie Stadium, Miami
MVP: 49ers WR Jerry Rice

January 22, 1984
L.A. Raiders 38, Washington 9
Tampa Stadium, Tampa
MVP: Raiders RB Marcus Allen

January 31, 1993
Dallas 52, Buffalo 17
Rose Bowl, Pasadena
MVP: Cowboys QB Troy Aikman

January 31, 1988
Washington 42, Denver 10
San Diego Jack Murphy Stadium, San Diego
MVP: Redskins QB Doug Williams

January 30, 1983
Washington 27, Miami 17
Rose Bowl, Pasadena
MVP: Redskins RB John Riggins

SUPER BOWL XVI

January 24, 1982
San Francisco 26, Cincinnati 21
Pontiac Silverdome, Pontiac
MVP: 49ers QB Joe Montana

SUPER BOWL XV

January 25, 1981
Oakland 27, Philadelphia 10
Louisiana Superdome, New Orleans
MVP: Raiders QB Jim Plunkett

Super Bowl XIV

January 20, 1980
Pittsburgh 31, Los Angeles 19
Rose Bowl, Pasadena
MVP: Steelers QB Terry Bradshaw

SUPER BOWL XIII

January 21, 1979
Pittsburgh 35, Dallas 31
Orange Bowl, Miami
MVP: Steelers QB Terry Bradshaw

SUPER BOWL XII

January 15, 1978
Dallas 27, Denver 10
Louisiana Superdome, New Orleans
MVPs: Cowboys DT Randy White
and DE Harvey Martin

SUPER BOWL XI

January 9, 1977
Oakland 32, Minnesota 14
Rose Bowl, Pasadena
MVP: Raiders WR Fred Biletnikoff

SUPER BOWL X

January 18, 1976
Pittsburgh 21, Dallas 17
Orange Bowl, Miami
MVP: Steelers WR Lynn Swann

SUPER BOWL IX

January 12, 1975
Pittsburgh 16, Minnesota 6
Tulane Stadium, New Orleans
MVP: Steelers RB Franco Harris

SUPER BOWL VIII

January 13, 1974
Miami 24, Minnesota 7
Rice Stadium, Houston
MVP: Dolphins RB Larry Csonka

SUPER BOWL VII

January 14, 1973
Miami 14, Washington 7
Memorial Coliseum, Los Angeles
MVP: Dolphins S Jake Scott

SUPER BOWL VI

January 16, 1972
Dallas 24, Miami 3
Tulane Stadium, New Orleans
MVP: Cowboys QB Roger Staubach

SUPER BOWL V

January 17, 1971
Baltimore 16, Dallas 13
Orange Bowl, Miami
MVP: Cowboys LB Chuck Howley

SUPER BOWL IV

January 11, 1970
Kansas City 23, Minnesota 7
Tulane Stadium, New Orleans
MVP: Chiefs QB Len Dawson

SUPER BOWL III

January 12, 1969
N.Y. Jets 16, Baltimore 7
Orange Bowl, Miami
MVP: Jets QB Joe Namath

SUPER BOWL II

January 14, 1968
Green Bay 33, Oakland 14
Orange Bowl, Miami
MVP: Packers QB Bart Starr

First World Championship Game AFL vs NFL

January 15, 1967
Green Bay 35, Kansas City 10
Memorial Coliseum, Los Angeles
MVP: Packers QB Bart Starr

The Vince Lombardi
Super Bowl Trophy

PLAYOFFS

Jeffrey Lurie
- Lazy Weekend Morning French Toast

Jeff Blake
- Baked Stuffed Mushrooms

Don Shula
- Hungarian Steak Soup

Kevin Carter
- Oxtail Stew With Vegetables
- Rice and Peas
- Fried Plantains

Lake Dawson
- Chicken Divan

Brett Favre
- Crawfish Étouffée

Robert Kraft
- Super Bowl Chili

Phil Simms
- Chicken Pot Pie

Emmitt Smith
- Sweet Potato Casserole

Brad Johnson
- Brad's Famous Lasagna

Steve Sabol
- Meat Loaf
- Green Beans With Red Bell Peppers
- Smashed Potatoes

Frank Gifford
- Hawaiian Chicken

Cornelius Bennett
- Shrimp Cornelius

Bill Tobin
- Raisin Pie

Desmond Howard
- Desmond's Mom's Caramel Cake

Desmond's Mom's Caramel Cake

Jeffrey Lurie

OWNER, PHILADELPHIA EAGLES

Following the purchase of the Eagles by film executive Lurie in 1994, Philadelphia has become a force again in the NFC East, qualifying for the playoffs in both 1995 and 1996. Lurie was named NFL owner of the year by *The Sporting News* in 1995 after his hiring of head coach Ray Rhodes (later named NFL coach of the year). Lurie served as the president and CEO of Chestnut Hill Productions in Los Angeles before assuming control of the Eagles.

A typical weekend morning in the Lurie household begins with this question: "When is Daddy coming down to make French toast?"

Jeffrey Lurie says he handles the weekend breakfast chores and the barbecuing. "But," he says, " everything in between is not my realm."

Lurie's French toast recipe originally was his mother's. "I've had an easier time making it since I've been in Philadelphia," he says.

"A local rabbi visits all the sports owners and the mayor, regardless of their ethnic backgrounds. He brings fresh challah every Friday."

Lazy Weekend Morning French Toast

1. Beat the eggs in a large bowl. Add the milk and vanilla and mix well.

2. Soak the bread slices thoroughly in the egg and milk mixture.

3. Preheat a griddle or frying pan. Lightly butter the pan or use a nonstick spray to coat. Fry the bread slices, pouring some of the remaining batter on each side before flipping.

4. Cook until each slice is golden brown on both sides.

5. Serve immediately, accompanied with pure maple syrup.

- 6 eggs
- ⅔ cup milk
- ¾ tsp vanilla
- 5 slices challah or sourdough bread, cut 1 ¼" thick

 EXTRA POINT: Challah is a Jewish egg bread, usually braided, that traditionally is baked on Fridays and for holidays. It is available at most delicatessens.

Jeff Blake

QUARTERBACK, CINCINNATI BENGALS

Cincinnati's Blake has emerged as one of the NFL's top young quarterbacks, a far cry from the beginning of his NFL career on the New York Jets' bench. In 1995, his first full season as a starter, Blake passed for 3,822 yards and 28 touchdowns and was voted to the Pro Bowl. He followed that with 3,624 yards and 24 touchdowns in 1996. Blake was selected in the sixth round of the 1992 NFL draft by the Jets. He joined the Bengals in 1994.

Lewanna Blake finds she cooks much more during the NFL season than the offseason. "During the season," she says, "Jeff comes home from work every day and we have dinner together. During the offseason, he travels a lot, going to charity events and so on. So we often just make something simple, such as hamburgers on the grill, or we go out or get takeout food. I have three young children, so when Jeff's gone, I'm too busy to cook." Lewanna likes to cook pastas with special sauces and anything nouvelle. *"I make the stuffed mushrooms when people come over, or when some of the Bengals' wives get together to watch a game," she says. "We have a lot of fun and it's not so lonely when the guys are on the road."*

- 1 package (8 oz) cream cheese, softened
- ¾ cup Parmesan cheese, freshly grated
- ¼ cup real bacon bits
- 2 cloves garlic, minced
- 20 medium mushroom caps
- 1 cup mild cheddar cheese, shredded

Baked Stuffed Mushrooms

1. Preheat oven to 375 degrees.

2. In a mixing bowl, blend the cream cheese, Parmesan, bacon bits, and garlic.

3. Spoon about a tablespoon of the mixture into each of the mushroom caps. Sprinkle the cheddar cheese on top.

4. Arrange the mushroom caps in a baking dish. Bake until the cheese is melted. Serve hot.

Jeff and Lewanna Blake

Don Shula

BALTIMORE COLTS 1963-69, MIAMI DOLPHINS 1970-1995

Pro Football Hall of Fame coach Shula won more games than any coach in NFL history (347). During his 33 years on the sideline with the Baltimore Colts (1963-69) and Miami Dolphins (1970-1995), Shula made a record six Super Bowl appearances. His 1972 Dolphins team had the only perfect season (17-0) in NFL history, capped by a victory in Super Bowl VII. Miami won Super Bowl VIII the following season. Shula also played in the NFL as a defensive back with Cleveland (1951-52), Baltimore (1953-56), and Washington (1957).

This is a dish from Don Shula's mother, who used to make it for him when he was a child. It is an authentic Hungarian recipe that Shula serves in five of his restaurants, including his flagship restaurant, Shula's Steak House, in Miami Lakes, Florida.

Hungarian Steak Soup

- 3-4 lbs steak or stew beef, cut into 1" cubes
- 4 large cloves garlic, finely chopped
- 3-4 carrots, diced
- 1 large onion, diced
- 3 stalks celery, diced
- 2½ Tbs paprika (Hungarian preferred)
- 1 ½ cans (6 oz each) tomato paste
- ¾ cup flour
- 6 cans (10 ½ oz) double strength beef stock
- 1 can (28 oz) tomato purée
- 2½ Tbs caraway seeds
- 1 Tbs dried oregano
- salt and pepper to taste

1. In a large, heavy-bottomed stew pot, sear the beef cubes on all sides. Add the garlic and sauté for a few minutes.

2. Add the carrots, onion, and celery and cook, stirring occasionally, until lightly browned. Add the paprika and cook for 5 minutes.

3. Add the tomato paste and then, gradually, the flour. Lower the heat to simmer and stir well while cooking. (The mixture in the pot will get thick and heavy; don't allow to burn on the bottom of the pot.)

4. Add the cans of stock and the cans of water as directed on the can labels and bring the pot to a boil. Reduce the heat and simmer for 10-15 minutes.

5. Add the tomato purée, caraway seeds, and oregano. Simmer, stirring occasionally, for 45 minutes. Adjust the seasoning with salt and pepper, and serve hot.

*Don Shula shows off the
pride of Shula's Steak House.*

Kevin Carter

DEFENSIVE END, ST. LOUIS RAMS

Carter, an All-America at Florida, came to the Rams as the sixth overall pick of the 1995 NFL draft. He started all 16 games in his rookie season, record- ed 6 sacks, and was honored by his teammates and coaches with the Carroll Rosenbloom Award, which is given to the Rams' rookie of the year. In 1996, Carter made 9½ sacks, second-highest total on the team.

Carter's wife Shima is from Jamaica, where she grew up eating the types of dishes she offers here, as cooked by her grandmother. "These recipes are typical Jamaican," she says. "I had to call my grandmother, who now lives in south Florida, to learn how to make them so I could introduce Kevin to Jamaican food. I've become better at cooking these dishes over time, and Kevin likes them a lot." What sets the rice and peas recipe apart from many similar bean and rice dishes is the coconut milk it is cooked in. "They call them red peas in Jamaica, not beans," Shima says. "And it's always called rice and peas, never peas and rice. I don't know why. That's just the way it is there."

Oxtail Stew With Vegetables

- 2 lbs (approx) oxtail, cut in ¾"-1" sections
- 2 Tbs soy sauce
- 2 medium cloves garlic, crushed
- 1 small onion, chopped
- salt and pepper, to taste
- 1 package (10-oz) frozen lima beans
- 12-16 baby carrots
- 1 medium onion, halved and sliced

1. Trim as much fat as possible from the oxtail sections. In a large bowl, combine the soy sauce, garlic, the small onion, and salt and pepper. Marinate the oxtail in the mixture for at least an hour.

2. In a deep (2-2½-inch) frying pan, pour 1 cup of water. Add the oxtail sections and cook over medium heat, turning the sections occasionally to cook evenly. Do not allow the water to cook away; keep adding to it as needed through the entire cooking process. Simmer the meat until tender, 3 hours or longer, skimming the fat every so often.

3. About 30 minutes before the meat is done, add the lima beans, carrots, and the medium onion to the pan. Continue cooking, adding small amounts of water as needed, until the vegetables are tender.

EXTRA POINT: This is an easy stew to make, but it does require attention during the lengthy cooking process. Shima suggests serving this with your favorite dumplings, which can be added to the pan to cook prior to adding the vegetables.

*Kevin and Shima Carter
fry plantains.*

Rice and Peas

1. Rinse and pick over the beans. Soak beans in water overnight. Or, cover the beans with water and bring to boil. Cover and let stand for 2 hours.

2. Drain the beans. In a large pot, cover the beans with water and boil until just tender, approximately 1 hour. Don't let the beans get too soft.

3. Add the coconut milk, thyme, scallion, and salt to the beans. Cook over low heat (do not allow to boil) for 15 minutes.

4. Add the rice to the pot along with enough water to equal about 2 cups of liquid in the pot. Stir and bring to a boil. Allow to boil for 1 to 2 minutes, then cover, and lower the heat to simmer. Cook until the rice is firm but tender, about 20 minutes. Stir once or twice to make sure the rice does not stick to the bottom of the pot.

- 8 oz dry small red beans
- 1 cup coconut milk (canned or frozen)
- 1 sprig thyme
- 1 scallion, chopped fine
- pinch of salt
- 1 cup white rice

Fried Plantains

- 1 ripe plantain
- 1 tsp vegetable oil

1. Peel the plantain. Cut the plantain into quarter-inch slices.

2. Fry the plantain slices in the oil until brown on both sides. Drain and serve.

 EXTRA POINT: Plantains are a type of large, starchy banana popular in the Caribbean and Central America. They are a tasty alternative to potatoes.

Lake Dawson

WIDE RECEIVER, KANSAS CITY CHIEFS

Dawson was the Chiefs' third-round pick in the 1994 NFL draft. In 1995, Dawson caught 40 passes for 524 yards and 5 touchdowns. Injuries shortened his 1996 season. He was a two-sport star (football and track) at Notre Dame, where he led the Irish in receptions in each of his last two seasons.

Chicken Divan

1. Preheat oven to 350 degrees.

2. In a large pot, cover the chicken with water and poach, partially covered, until just cooked through, about 15-20 minutes. Drain well.

3. Cover the bottom of a well-greased 9" x 13" pan with the cooked broccoli. Layer the cooked chicken on top of the broccoli.

4. In a large mixing bowl, combine the mayonnaise, soups, 1 cup of the cheddar cheese, lemon juice, and curry powder. Mix well.

5. Pour the sauce mixture over the chicken. Sprinkle with the bread crumbs, then with the remaining cheddar cheese. Bake for 25 minutes.

- 3-4 large chicken breasts, skinned and boned
- 2 packages (10 oz each) frozen broccoli, cooked and well drained
- 1 cup mayonnaise
- 1 can (10¾ oz) cream of chicken soup
- 1 can (10¾ oz) cream of mushroom soup
- 1 ½ cups cheddar cheese
- 1 tsp lemon juice
- ½ tsp curry powder
- bread crumbs

Brett Favre

QUARTERBACK, GREEN BAY PACKERS

Brett Favre capped a storybook 1996 season by passing for 2 touchdowns and rushing for another in the Packers' 35-21 victory over New England in Super Bowl XXXI. Favre has emerged as one of the NFL's top quarterbacks, winning NFL MVP honors from *Associated Press* in 1995 and 1996. In 1996, he passed for 39 touchdowns, breaking the club record of 38 he established in 1995. Favre was drafted by Atlanta in 1991. Green Bay acquired him in a trade in 1992.

For the Packers' annual Christmas party, Brett and Deanna Favre make one of their signature Southern specialty dishes. Deanna tells this story about the 1996 party. "We decided we would make Shrimp Creole," she says. "I went out shopping for all the ingredients. And, while Brett was at practice, I prepared the dish—peeled, cut, and cooked all the shrimp and so on. When Brett got home, I was tired and went upstairs to change clothes for the party. While I was getting ready, Brett mixed the prepared ingredients together and put the shrimp creole in a serving dish. When we got to the party, Brett immediately called everyone's attention to the great dish he had prepared, which just confirmed for me that behind every great man, there is an even better woman."

- **1 stick margarine**
- **2 green bell peppers, chopped**
- **2-3 stalks of celery, chopped**
- **1 large onion, chopped**
- **3-4 cans (10¾ oz each) cream of mushroom soup**
- **1 lb crawfish tails**
- **2 cans (10 oz) diced tomatoes with green chiles, undrained**
- **cooked white rice**

Crawfish Étouffée

1. In a large pot or cast iron Dutch oven, melt the margarine and sauté the peppers, celery, and onion.

2. Add the soup and cook over low heat, stirring occasionally, for 20-30 minutes.

3. Add the crawfish tails and cook for 30-40 minutes more.

4. Add the tomatoes and their liquid, and stir to blend completely. Serve over rice in individual serving bowls.

Brett and Deanna Favre

Robert Kraft

OWNER, NEW ENGLAND PATRIOTS

Kraft, a Boston native, purchased the Patriots in 1994. Three seasons later, the Patriots won the AFC championship and played in Super Bowl XXXI. Kraft, who played football at Columbia University, had previous sports and franchise ownership experience. In the 1970s, he owned the Boston Lobsters professional tennis team. Along with the Patriots and Foxboro Stadium, Kraft owns the Rand-Whitney Group, Inc., and International Forest Products, one of the largest privately owned paper and packaging companies in the United States.

This chili recipe makes enough for a Super Bowl party, according to Kraft's wife Myra. It serves approximately 35 people, and can be accompanied with bowls of finely chopped white onion, grated cheddar cheese, and sour cream to use as toppings. Myra also suggests serving the chili with a green salad and sliced sourdough bread.

- ½ cup olive oil
- 1¾ lbs yellow onions, coarsely chopped
- 2 lbs sweet Italian sausage, casings removed
- 8 lbs lean ground beef
- 1½ Tbs fresh-ground black pepper, or to taste
- 2 cans (12 oz each) tomato paste
- 5 Tbs garlic, minced
- 3 oz ground cumin seed
- 4 oz chili powder
- ½ cup Dijon mustard
- 4 Tbs salt
- 4 Tbs dried basil
- 4 Tbs dried oregano
- 5 cans (35 oz each) Italian plum tomatoes
- ½ cup dry red wine
- ¼ cup lemon juice
- ½ cup fresh dill, chopped
- ½ cup fresh Italian parsley, chopped
- ½ cup fresh cilantro, chopped
- 3 cans (16 oz each) dark red kidney beans

Super Bowl Chili

1. Heat the olive oil in a very large soup kettle. Add the onions and cook over low heat, covered, until tender and translucent, about 10 minutes.

2. Raise the heat to medium and add the sausage meat and ground beef. Stir often until the meat is completely browned.

3. Drain off as much fat as possible.

4. Reduce the heat to low. Stir in the black pepper, tomato paste, garlic, cumin, chili powder, mustard, salt, basil, and oregano.

5. Drain the tomatoes and add to the pot with the red wine, lemon juice, dill, parsley, and cilantro. Drain the kidney beans and add them to the pot. Stir well. Simmer, uncovered, for 15 minutes. Taste and correct the seasoning. If you like your chili spicier, add more chili powder to taste.

Phil Simms

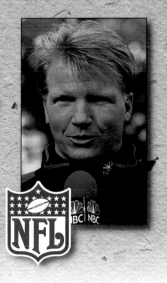

QUARTERBACK, NEW YORK GIANTS (1979-1993)

In 1986, quarterback Simms led the Giants to a 14-2 record and victory in Super Bowl XXI. In that game, he completed a Super Bowl-record 88 percent of his passes (22 of 25) for 268 yards and 3 touchdowns, to earn Most Valuable Player honors. During his 15-year career in New York, he became the fourteenth quarterback in NFL history to pass for more than 30,000 yards. Simms currently works as an analyst for NBC Sports.

"My wife Diana, who is a very good cook, can't believe I picked this recipe to include in this cookbook," says Phil Simms.

"But it's simple to prepare, and it's the favorite of our kids."

Chicken Pot Pie

1. Preheat oven to 325 degrees.

2. Cut the carrots and celery into bite-sized pieces. Peel and dice the potatoes.

3. Boil the chicken in a medium saucepan until tender (about 20 minutes). Remove the chicken from the pan, reserving the stock, and allow to cool. Discard the skin and bones, then cut the chicken into bite-sized pieces.

4. Boil the vegetables in the reserved stock until tender. Drain the vegetables and place them with the chicken in an ovenproof bowl.

5. In a small saucepan, heat the soup and milk together, stirring until warm and well blended. Pour over the chicken and vegetables.

6. Cover the bowl with the pie crust and crimp the edges to seal. Bake until the crust is golden brown, approximately 45 minutes.

- 4 carrots
- 4 celery stalks
- 6 medium potatoes
- 3 chicken breasts
- 1 can (10¾ oz) cream of chicken soup
- 1 cup skim milk
- 1 9-inch pie crust

EXTRA POINT: A dash of cayenne pepper or paprika can be added for a slightly spicier dish.

Emmitt Smith

RUNNING BACK, DALLAS COWBOYS

In seven seasons, Smith has won four NFL rushing titles and played in three Super Bowl victories (XXVII, XXVIII, and XXX). The phenomenal running back won league most-valuable-player honors in 1993, the same season he earned MVP honors in the Cowboys' Super Bowl XXVIII triumph. In 1995, Smith's 25 rushing touchdowns established an NFL record.

"This recipe is dynamite," Smith says. "It's a great side dish to serve at family dinners during the holidays."

- 6-8 large sweet potatoes
- 1 egg
- 1 cup sugar
- 1 stick butter or margarine, melted
- 2 Tbs flour
- ½ cup evaporated milk
- 1 ½ tsp cinnamon
- 1 tsp allspice
- 1 ½ tsp vanilla

TOPPING:
- 1 stick butter or margarine
- 2 cups brown sugar
- 2 cups pecan pieces

Sweet Potato Casserole

1. Preheat oven to 350 degrees. In a large pot, boil the potatoes with skins on until they are soft. Let the potatoes cool.

2. Remove the skins from the potatoes and place them in a large mixing bowl. Whip the potatoes with an electric mixer until smooth. Add the egg, sugar, butter, flour, and evaporated milk and mix well to blend. Add the spices and vanilla, and mix well.

3. Make the topping by first melting the butter or margarine in a medium saucepan over low heat. Add the brown sugar and pecans and stir until the mixture is smooth and easy to spread.

4. Spread the potatoes in a 9" x 13" glass baking dish. Spread the topping evenly over the potatoes. Bake for 40 minutes.

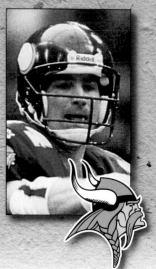

Brad Johnson

QUARTERBACK, MINNESOTA VIKINGS

Johnson directed the Vikings to a 4-2 record in the final six games of 1996 and helped them achieve a wild-card playoff berth. In eight starts for Minnesota, Johnson passed for 2,258 yards and 17 touchdowns. He finished third among NFL quarterbacks in 1996 with an 89.4 passer rating—behind only San Francisco's Steve Young and Green Bay's Brett Favre. Johnson was a ninth-round draft pick out of Florida State in 1992.

- 2 Tbs extra virgin olive oil
- 2 lbs Italian sausage (mild or hot, to taste), casings removed
- 2 lbs ground sirloin
- 4 medium cloves garlic, minced
- 2 cans (6 oz each) tomato paste
- 2 cans (28 oz each) tomato puree
- 1 can (28 oz) crushed tomatoes, plus 1 can water
- 2-3 Tbs fresh basil, chopped
- 2-3 Tbs fresh oregano, chopped
- 3 Tbs sugar
- 3 chicken bouillon cubes
- 3 beef bouillon cubes
- 1 cup dry red wine
- 2 cups Romano cheese, freshly grated
- salt and pepper to taste
- 2 lbs ricotta cheese
- 1 egg, beaten
- ½ tsp garlic powder
- 1 lb lasagna noodles, cooked and separated
- 2 cups mozzarella cheese, shredded

Brad's Famous Lasagna

1. In a large frying pan, brown the sausage, ground sirloin, and garlic in the olive oil.

2. Add the tomato paste, tomato purée, and the crushed tomatoes. Stir to blend.

3. Add the can of water, the basil, oregano, sugar, bouillon cubes, wine, and 1 cup of the Romano cheese. Add salt and pepper to taste. Stir and simmer for 1 hour.

4. In a large mixing bowl, make the cheese filling by mixing the ricotta cheese, the beaten egg, one-half cup of the Romano cheese, the garlic powder, and a dash of salt and pepper to taste. Blend thoroughly.

5. Preheat oven to 400 degrees. In a 12" x 14" baking pan or dish, spread enough of the tomato sauce to cover the bottom of the dish. Next, line the dish with a layer of lasagna noodles. Then, spread some of the cheese filling over the noodles. Finally, sprinkle with some of the remaining half-cup of the Romano cheese and some of the mozzarella cheese. Repeat these layers until the pan is filled. Top with the last of the tomato sauce, sprinkled with the last of the Romano and mozzarella cheese.

6. Bake for 25 minutes or until the cheese is completely melted.

Steve Sabol

PRESIDENT, NFL FILMS

Steve Sabol has been involved in capturing NFL action for 35 years. Of the 69 Emmy Awards NFL Films has won, 26 have gone to Sabol for his writing, editing, directing, and producing. Sabol, a former All-Rocky Mountain Conference running back for Colorado College, serves as the host of *NFL Films Presents*, the longest-running syndicated sports series on television.

Steve Sabol allows himself to stay home and be a football spectator one weekend a season. "During the championship-game weekend, I just sit down in front of the TV and watch," he says. "And this is my favorite meal for that weekend. It is definitely a cold-weather meal—substantial enough to get you through a playoff doubleheader." These recipes come from Penny Ashman, Sabol's long-time companion. "Penny does the real cooking," Sabol says. "My job with the meat loaf is to shmush together all the ingredients. I'm definitely unskilled labor."

- ¼ cup carrots, finely chopped
- 1 cup celery, chopped
- 1 onion, chopped
- 3 Tbs butter
- 1 ½ lbs ground sirloin
- ¾ lb ground pork
- ¾ lb ground veal
- ½ cup fresh parsley, finely chopped
- ⅓ cup sour cream
- ½ cup bread crumbs
- ¼ tsp dried thyme
- ¼ tsp marjoram
- salt and pepper to taste
- 1 egg
- 1 Tbs Worcestershire sauce
- ½ cup bottled chili sauce
- 2 slices bacon

Meat Loaf

1. Preheat oven to 350 degrees. Oil an 8" x 4" loaf pan.
2. In a heavy skillet over medium heat, sauté the carrots, celery, and onion in butter until soft (about 5 minutes). Scrape into a large mixing bowl and cool.
3. When cool, combine the vegetables with the ground meats, parsley, sour cream, bread crumbs, thyme, marjoram, salt, and pepper. Whisk the egg with the Worcestershire and chili sauces, then add to the meat mixture. Using your hands, mix well. Form into a loaf.
4. Place the meat loaf in the oiled loaf pan. Top with the bacon slices and bake about 1 hour or until top is browned. Slice and serve.

 EXTRA POINT: One of the best things about many holiday-season meals is the leftovers. The meat loaf makes wonderful sandwiches.

- **2 Tbs olive oil**
- **2 cloves garlic, minced**
- **1 red bell pepper, seeded, cored, and sliced into 1" x ½" pieces**
- **1 lb fresh green beans**
- **2 Tbs fresh basil, chopped**
- **juice from ½ lemon**
- **salt and pepper to taste**

Green Beans With Red Bell Peppers

1. In a large skillet, heat the olive oil over medium heat.

2. Add the peppers and garlic; stir. Add the green beans and basil. Sauté for 4-5 minutes, stirring occasionally.

3. Add the lemon juice, salt, and pepper. Lower the heat, cover, and cook until the green beans are tender, about 2 to 3 minutes.

Smashed Potatoes

1. Fill a large pot three-quarters full with cold water. Add the potatoes, salt, and garlic. Bring the water to a boil and cook until the potatoes are tender when pierced with a fork, about 15 minutes.

2. Reserve one-third cup of boiling water from the potatoes, then drain the potatoes in a colander.

3. Return the potatoes to the pot and turn heat to low. Smash the potatoes with a potato masher. Add butter, reserved water, and Worcestershire sauce. Continue mashing until the ingredients are blended. Add the half & half and cheese. Mash until the potatoes are creamy. Mix in the pepper, parsley, and chives. Cover and heat for 5 minutes. Serve immediately.

- **2 lbs white, red, yellow, or baking potatoes, partially peeled and cut into 2" chunks**
- **1 tsp salt**
- **1 clove garlic, whole**
- **4 Tbs butter**
- **⅓ cup water (from boiled potatoes)**
- **½ tsp Worcestershire sauce**
- **⅓ cup half & half**
- **¼ cup cheddar cheese, grated**
- **pepper to taste**
- **2 Tbs fresh parsley, chopped**
- **2 Tbs fresh chives, chopped**

Frank Gifford

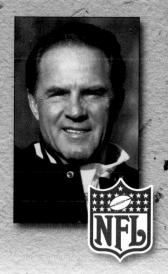

HALFBACK/FLANKER, NEW YORK GIANTS 1952-1960, 1962-64
Football fans born after 1971 may know Gifford only as an analyst in ABC's *Monday Night Football* booth. However, the former All-America from USC had a stellar 12-year career as a halfback and flanker for the Giants. Gifford, a member of the Pro Football Hall of Fame, was named to seven Pro Bowls. He was *United Press* NFL player of the year in 1956, when he helped lead the Giants to the NFL championship. Gifford began his broadcast career in 1957. He joined ABC in 1971, the second season of the Monday night telecasts.

Grilled Hawaiian Chicken

1. In a bowl large enough to hold both the prepared marinade and chicken, mix the soy sauce and sugars with a whisk. Add the rice vinegar, ginger root, and pineapple and blend well.

2. Add the skinless chicken parts.

3. Marinate 1 to 6 hours. Refrigerate if marinating more than 1 hour. Do not marinate the chicken for more than 6 hours.

4. Grill the chicken until tender.

- **Up to 20 pieces skinless chicken (thighs, drumsticks, and breasts recommended)**
  MARINADE:
- **4 cups soy sauce**
- **1 cup granulated sugar**
- **1 cup brown sugar**
- **2 cups mild rice vinegar**
- **2 cups ginger root, sliced**
- **1 can (12 oz) crushed pineapple**

 EXTRA POINT: The amount of sugar in the marinade may be increased or decreased to your personal taste.

Cornelius Bennett

LINEBACKER, ATLANTA FALCONS

Bennett has played in five Pro Bowls and four Super Bowls—all with the Buffalo Bills. The second overall selection of the 1987 NFL draft, he had a standout college career at Alabama, where he became the first linebacker to win the Vince Lombardi Trophy as the nation's top collegiate lineman. Bennett spent nine seasons with Buffalo, then went to Atlanta as a free agent in 1996.

Bennett says his cooking philosophy is a lot like his football philosophy. "If you don't try something new," he says, "you can't be success-ful. On the football field, I try to be creative to be successful. It's the same in the kitchen—you can't be afraid to try anything." Bennett, who loves to cook, but hates doing the dishes afterward, adds, "To me, the most important thing in cooking is preparation. Have all your ingredients in front of you before you begin."

- 1 lb linguine
- 8 oz light Italian salad dressing
- 1 zucchini, cut in matchstick strips
- 1 carrot, cut in matchstick strips
- 4 green onions, chopped
- 2 Tbs fresh parsley, finely chopped
- 2 tsp lemon zest, grated
- ⅛ tsp fresh cracked black pepper
- 1 lb shrimp, cleaned and peeled
- grated Parmesan cheese to taste, optional

Shrimp Cornelius

1. Bring the water for the pasta to a boil in a large covered pot. Uncover the pot and cook linguine according to the package directions.
2. While the linguine is cooking, heat the salad dressing in a large deep skillet over medium heat. Add the zucchini, carrots, green onions, parsley, lemon zest, and black pepper. Cook until the vegetables are crisp-tender, about five minutes.
3. Add the shrimp and cook until done (when they turn bright pink).
4. Drain the linguine, then add it to the shrimp and vegetables and heat through, tossing gently. Sprinkle with Parmesan cheese and serve immediately.

Bill Tobin

VICE PRESIDENT/DIRECTOR OF FOOTBALL OPERATIONS, INDIANAPOLIS COLTS

In Bill Tobin's first three seasons as the Colts' vice president and director of football operations, Indianapolis has reached the playoffs twice, including an appearance in the 1995 AFC Championship Game. He previously spent 18 seasons in the Chicago Bears' front office. Along with his almost three decades of NFL management experience, Tobin has solid playing credentials. As a running back, he was the Houston Oilers' rookie of the year in 1963.

There is a story behind this pie. "The favorite pie of my grandfather, Duke Vunovich, always has been raisin," says Bill's wife, Dusene. "He insisted on having it at family Thanksgivings along with the other more traditional pies. Over a few days he managed to eat the entire pie because no one else in the family liked it. He often bribed the grandchildren and others to take a bite. Over time, it became a family favorite. And now he complains that everyone eats his pie."

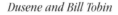

Dusene and Bill Tobin

Raisin Pie

1. Preheat oven to 425 degrees. Place the raisins in a saucepan.

2. Mix together the brown and white sugar and the flour. Add the mixture to the pan with the raisins and stir well.

3. Pour in the hot water. Over high heat, bring the raisin mixture to a boil. Stir continuously as the mixture thickens.

4. Remove the pan from the heat and stir in the lemon juice. Cool the pan in a bath of cold water in the sink. Stir occasionally as the raisin filling cools.

5. Pour the raisin filling into the unbaked pie shell. Add the top crust (lattice top is suggested).

6. Bake for 30-45 minutes, or long enough to brown the top crust.

- 2½ cups raisins
- ¼ cup brown sugar
- ¼ cup white sugar
- 3 tablespoons flour
- 2 cups hot water
- 3 Tbs concentrated lemon juice
- 1 double pie crust, unbaked

Desmond Howard

WIDE RECEIVER/KICK RETURNER, OAKLAND RAIDERS

Howard was named the Most Valuable Player of Super Bowl XXXI. He returned a kickoff 99 yards for a touchdown and tied the Super Bowl record for most combined yards gained in a game (244) in Green Bay's 35-21 victory over New England. Howard won the Heisman Trophy at Michigan in 1991, then was drafted by Washington, where he played three seasons. He spent a year with Jacksonville before going to Green Bay in 1996. Howard signed with the Raiders as a free agent in the 1997 offseason.

Desmond Howard's mother, Hattie Charles (also known to her family as Aunt Hattie), says her sons are "superb cooks." "Desmond even surprised me one time by flying in to see me just so he could learn how to make pasta from scratch," she says. The caramel cake recipe here, one of Desmond's favorites, is so good it even moved Desmond's older brother Jonathan to poetry: "Aunt Hattie's caramel cake/It's not shake and bake/or even fake./But after a slice of it,/you'll have the temptation/to shake, fake, and break/your way into a league of your own/or any zone."

CAKE:
- 2 cups (4 sticks) unsalted butter, at room temperature (plus a bit more for greasing the cake pans)
- 3 cups sifted all-purpose flour (plus more for the cake pans)
- 1 Tbs. baking powder
- 1 Tbs. cocoa
- 2 cups sugar
- 2 tsp vanilla extract
- 6 large eggs, at room temperature
- 1 cup milk
- 1 cup toasted pecans, chopped (optional)

CARAMEL ICING:
- 1 cup (2 sticks) unsalted butter, cut into 8 pieces
- 1 lb light brown sugar
- 1 cup granulated sugar
- 1 can 12-oz evaporated milk

Desmond's Mom's Caramel Cake

1. Preheat oven to 350 degrees. Lightly grease and flour three 8-inch round cake pans and set aside.

2. Sift the flour, baking powder, and cocoa together and set aside. Cream the butter and sugar together in the bowl of an electric mixer at medium speed until the mixture is light and fluffy. Add the vanilla. Beat in the eggs one at a time. Change the mixer speed to low and add the dry ingredients alternately with the milk, a little at a time. Mix just until the ingredients are blended. (Overmixing will make the cake tough.)

3. Divide the batter among the prepared cake pans. Bake until a toothpick inserted in the center of each layer comes out clean, about 20-25 minutes. Place the pans on a wire rack to cool.

4. After about 20 minutes, remove the cake layers from the pans and let them cool completely. When the layers are cool, make the frosting.

5. Place one layer on a plate and spread it with about one-fourth of the icing. If using pecans, sprinkle on the icing. Top with a second cake layer and spread it with the same amount of icing and optional pecans. Top with the

Desmond Howard and his mother, Hattie Charles

remaining cake layer. Frost the top and sides of the cake with the remaining icing and sprinkle on pecans. Let the cake set at least 1½ hours before serving.

6. To make the icing, stir together all the ingredients—butter, sugar, and evaporated milk—in a medium-heavy saucepan over low heat.

7. Cook, stirring constantly, until the sugar is completely dissolved and the icing is thick.

8. To test if the icing is ready, drop one-half teaspoonful of it into a glass of cold water; it is ready when it forms a soft ball.

Official ⬤NFL⬤ Cooking Signals

Here are a few NFL officials' signals from the playing field adapted for some kitchen fun.
What the signals actually mean is below each caption in parentheses.

Preheat
the Oven
(First Down)

Mix Well
(False Start, Illegal Formation, or Kick Off Out of Bounds)

Refrigerate
Overnight
(Delay of Game or Excess Time Out)

Stir Constantly
(No Time Out or Time In With Whistle)

Easy on
the Spices
(Holding)

Separate the Eggs
(Pass Juggled Inbounds and Caught Out of Bounds)

Shake Well
(Intentional Grounding of Pass)

Low-Fat Dish
(Offside, Encroachment, Neutral Zone Infraction)

Chop Coarsely
(Illegal Cut, Illegal Block Below the Waist, Clipping)

Mince
(Illegal Crackback Block)

Optional Ingredient
(Player Disqualified)

Season to Taste
(Facemask)

Roll Out the Dough
(Illegal Shift)

Bring to a Boil
(Reset Play Clock— 40 Seconds)

Dinner Time!
(Touchdown, Field Goal, or Successful Extra-Point Try)

More, Please
(Crowd Noise, Dead Ball, or Neutral Zone Established)

NFL PARTY TIPS

With *THE NFL FAMILY COOKBOOK*, an NFL Party Never Is Out of Season

You don't have to wait for Super Sunday to have an NFL-themed celebration. The NFL calendar presents football party opportunities all year long—Draft Day get-togethers in April, autumn tailgate feasts at the stadium, summertime picnics at your favorite team's training camp site, or casual get-togethers at home in front of the TV for an NFL Sunday doubleheader. All that is required is a little imagination and a good party game plan. Don't forget that the NFL season overlaps the major holidays (Labor Day, Thanksgiving, Christmas, and New Year's Eve), giving you even more reasons to celebrate. And then there is the Super Bowl, which has become an unofficial national holiday.

As with all parties, NFL parties work best if most of the kitchen work is done before your guests arrive. Choose the recipes you are going to serve to allow yourself as much time with your guests as possible. Many of the recipes in The NFL Family Cookbook *can be prepared the night before a party, then served the next day either at room temperature or reheated. Some recipes also can be partially prepared ahead and refrigerated, then finished an hour or so before serving. But try to stay away from leaving yourself too much cooking to do when the party starts. After all, would you rather be in the kitchen working or watching the game? And, because many NFL-themed gatherings are outdoor events in warm weather, remember to follow safe food-handling guidelines and choose dishes that safely can be left unrefrigerated for a limited time.*

One of the nice things about NFL parties is that they lend themselves to colorful decorations. Extend the excitement of the game to your party by introducing the colors of your favorite team into your tableware, napkins, and party-design scheme. Many NFL licensees produce official team- and Super Bowl–identified party decorations, and tailgating and at-home items, including coolers, aprons, and oven mitts, dinnerware, serving pieces, barbecues, and cutting boards. (To find out "where to buy it," see the list of major retailers that carry official NFL kitchen and party merchandise on page 156.)

The recipes in The NFL Family Cookbook *can be mixed and matched in a delicious variety of ways: by season (for example, summer luncheons and down-home picnics), by type of cuisine (such as Cajun or Mexican), or by style of event (for instance, a stadium tailgate barbecue or an elegant postseason dinner party). Here are a dozen NFL party ideas to get you started, including sample menus that use the recipes in this book.*

Draft-Day Brunch

Good and Hearty Bran Muffins (page 39)
Saturday Morning Waffles (page 95) or...
Lazy Weekend Morning French Toast (page 127)
Grits With Sausage and Eggs (page 13)
Apple Bundt Cake (page 42)

Down-Home Training Camp Blow-Out

Texas Caviar (page 52)
Johnnie's Drummetes (page 80)
Deacon's Pork Salad (page 26)
Down Home Macaroni and Cheese (page 31)
Sweet Potato Pie (page 23)

Tailgate Barbecue

Tailgate Corn Salad (page 83)

Baby Back, Back, Back Ribs (page 67)

Marinated Flank Steak (page 86)

Barbecued Baked Beans (page 26)

Peanut Butter Cup Pie (page 81)

Crunchy Chocolate Chip Cookies (page 87)

Monday Night House Party

Cheese Loaf (page 65)

Brad's Famous Lasagna (page 142)

Hawaiian Chicken (page 147)

Pumpkin Bars (page 119)

Kangaroo Cookies (page 110)

The NFL Family Cookbook Chili Cook-Off

Chicken Salsa Chili (page 77)

Tom Matte's Chili (page 118)

Super Bowl Chili

(page 138)

Cajun Bash

Cajun Shrimp Appetizer (page 16)

Diana's Creamy Coleslaw (page 69)

Tony's Shrimp Gumbo (page 70)

Smothered Chicken (page 17)

Crawfish Étouffée (page 136)

Cornbread Muffins (page 24)

Texas Sheet Cake (page 73)

Sunday Night Italian Buffet

Vegetable Pizza (page 41)

Italian Sausage Soup With Tortellini

(page 114)

Low-Fat Eggplant Parmesan (page 43)

Pasta With Sun-Dried Tomatoes and

Greens (page 66)

Zucchini Proudone (page 101)

Moist Chocolate Cake (page 88)

Backyard Beach Party

Jamaican Jerk Chicken (page 72)

Grilled Mahi Mahi With Spicy

Pineapple Relish (page 76)

Fried Plantains (page 134)

Rice and Peas (page 134)

Banana Nut Bread (page 33)

Thanksgiving Weekend Football Feast

Baked Stuffed Mushrooms (page 128)

Orange Raisin Glazed Ham (page 24)

Pheasant and Wild Rice Casserole

(page 111)

Broccoli and Macaroni Hollandaise

(page 68)

Sweet Potato Casserole (page 140)

Apple Pie (page 120)

Raisin Pie (page 149)

Football Fiesta

Salsa Pico de Gallo (page 66)

Quarterback Stew (page 99)

Beef Flautas (page 45)

Chicken Chile Rellenos (page 112)

Lemon Squares (page 83)

Elegant Playoff Weekend Dinner Party

Hungarian Steak Soup (page 130)

Barbecued Salmon Salad With

Sun-Dried Tomato Vinaigrette

(page 74)

Dijon Chicken With Gorgonzola

(page 84)

Green Beans With Red Bell

Peppers (page 145)

Yeast Rolls (page 54)

Desmond's Mom's Caramel Cake

(page 150)

Preseason Patio Luncheon

Easy Shrimp Dip (page 98)

Blueberry Spinach Salad (page 65)

Summer Risotto (page 78)

Crunchy Coffee Frozen Torte (page 59)

Where to Buy NFL Kitchen Items

Here is a list of major retailers that carry NFL products with a kitchen theme:

Bed, Bath & Beyond

Carson Pirie Scott

Champs

Federated

Host Marriott (*airport shops*)

Kmart

Kohl's

Linens 'n Things

May Company

Mercantile

Montgomery Ward (*catalog*)

Paradies (*airport shops*)

JC Penney

Pro Image

QVC (*home shopping channel*)

Sears

Service Merchandise (*catalog*)

Shopko

W. H. Smith (*airport shops*)

Spiegel (*catalog*)

The Sports Authority

Target

Wal-Mart

Having a Super Bowl Party?
Invite *The Official Super Bowl Game Program*!

The Official Super Bowl Game Program is the ultimate party favor for at-home Super Bowl celebrations. And, now, you can order it by the carton for delivery *before* the big game! The same official game program sold at the Super Bowl stadium, it brings all the color and excitement of Super Sunday to your party. Call toll-free for information and to order *The Official Super Bowl Game Program* with a credit card: 1-800-NFL-1721.

RECIPE INDEX

Photo Credits: